365 TO VISION

MODERN WRITER'S GUIDE

(HOW TO PRODUCE MORE QUALITY WRITING IN LESS TIME)

RON LIEBACK

Copyright Page:

First paperback edition August 2020

Book design by Ebook Launch

Edited by Miranda Miller

Cover Logo by Ange Valenti

ISBN 978-1-7355588-0-6 (paperback)
ISBN 978-1-7355588-1-3 (ebook)

Some material used in this book first appeared in *Search Engine Journal* and *Forbes.*

365toVision.com

Dedication Page

Dedicated to writers and editors everywhere.

Endless thanks to my editor Miranda Miller and logo designer Ange Valenti. Also, thanks to all the editors, writers, educators, and entrepreneurs I have worked with throughout the years. And of course, a huge thanks to my wife Pam and son Enzo, two people who understand and support my passion for not only the written word, but entrepreneurism.

CONTENTS

FOREWORD

Once upon a time, in the pre-Internet world, I occasionally used to blindly take a chance on a new band or a new album, based on a friend's recommendation or a great review in a magazine. Every once in a while, I'd stumble upon something truly excellent that just blew away my expectations and stayed in my listening rotation for years.

In November 2017, I received my first email from Ron Lieback. He was trying to find a platform where he could write about topics like content marketing, SEO, and business development. In my role of Executive Editor of *Search Engine Journal*, I see hundreds of these requests every month – people wanting to write for our popular industry publication.

It's easy to get jaded as you read these pitches. As good as they sometimes seem, you never know what you're actually going to get. Most people give up after one pitch. That's where many people mess up – a lack of persistence.

Eventually, in January 2018, I responded to Ron and we agreed on his first topic. Once he submitted his first post, I instantly realized what a talented writer he was. It was entirely painless editing his work – and believe me when I type this: this is rarely the case for an editor! As a result, I quickly added him as a regular contributor, writing monthly at *Search Engine Journal*.

I still recall later in the fall of 2018 talking to Web Traffic Advisors[1] founder Chris Boggs, the person who recommended Ron reach out to me about writing for *Search Engine Journal*, and thanked him for pointing Ron my way. My praise for Ron's writing was effusive.

As of this writing, Ron has written nearly 30 articles on *Search Engine Journal*. All of Ron's articles have provided countless insights and tips for our audience of SEO and marketing professionals – but it is in articles on writing well, creativity, and his own personal processes and habits that have been among my personal favorites. (It's also where I feel like Ron truly shines brightest.)

In particular, his "11 Habits of Content Creators Who Optimize 'Creative Spend'"[2] should be required reading for any writer or content creator. In today's world, it is so easy to get distracted – arguing on Facebook, responding to text messages, writing emails, and countless other online rabbit holes.

But maintaining focus, keeping your energy high, and making sure your mind is sharp are so crucial when creating. It's incredibly hard to do this every day, but having healthy routines and rituals – the kind Ron advocates – is something we all need to strive for to be at our best.

---

1 https://www.webtrafficadvisors.com/

2 https://www.searchenginejournal.com/11-habits-of-content-creators-who-optimize-creative-spend/299863/

Nobody is born an amazing writer, just as nobody is born with an athletic body. And there is no "magic bullet" that will help you instantly become an exceptional writer. However, Ron's book will tell you exactly what you need to do. You'll just need to follow the advice and find what works for you.

I hear one question more than any other: "How can I improve my writing?" Well, thankfully now I have a great resource from a marketer whom I trust that I can send people to to answer such a deep question.

Writing is hard – but so is trying to run a marathon when you've never trained before or trying to play your favorite song when you've just picked up a guitar for the first time. To steal a quote from Billy Beane (as portrayed by Brad Pitt) in "Moneyball," writing "is a process, it's a process, it's a process."

And the writing process becomes infinitely more fun and rewarding when you've trained your mind and body and you start pumping out winning content every time your fingers touch the keys.

To circle back to where we started, Ron Lieback was that metaphorical "band" I took a chance on. He has blown away my expectations and remains on my must-listen playlist. I hope what you're about to read blows you away and helps you learn how to improve your writing through a proven process. Happy reading!

- Danny Goodwin, Executive Editor, *Search Engine Journal*

Introduction

"In my dreams, crowds were chanting, challenging me, shouting, 'Follow us and fit in!' I wanted to tell him that life itself has turned into a prowling lion. I wanted to tell him that I needed to escape the blaze of bullshit."
— Bob Dylan, Chronicles: Volume One

"Money talks, bullshit walks."
— Stephen King, The Drawing of the Three

Let me share a quick secret: writer's block is pure BS.

The proverbial writer's block is the number one excuse so many stalled-out modern writers turn to when they're having trouble producing anything valuable or readable.

For those *want-to-be* freelancers, writer's block can become a too-convenient excuse for the inability to earn enough money to sustain a living by writing.

A lot of people get into writing as a pathway to the type of lifestyle it can provide; one that doesn't adhere to the archaic 9-to-5 working world.

This craving was real for modern writers long before the COVID-19 pandemic forced millions to work from home, though this "new norm" has now affected thousands of companies. Some as big as Twitter now offer a full-time work-at-home lifestyle.

Many of these workers create content.

Wherever you are at in your writing career and however you got there, how can you maximize your skills and situation to produce the best end product possible?

A belief in writer's block is just one element that can prevent you from writing well and often. Maybe you find it difficult to get motivated, or haven't designed a real process to help you do your best work.

You obviously care about writing well, or you wouldn't be reading this. This is exactly why I wrote *365 to Vision: Modern Writer's Guide, How to Produce More Quality Writing in Less Time*. In sharing my own experiences and the lessons I've learned from great writers along the way, I hope to provide the tools and routines you need to seriously improve your writing.

This book addresses not only the essentials of modern writing like craft, form, and routine, but also the productive lifestyle habits demanded of the modern writer.

I'm not asking you to master the art of writing—that takes a lot more time and practice than you'll find in any one book. Rather, I want to help you master the *process of writing consistently* so you can produce quality and valuable content on a regular basis.

This title follows the "365 to Vision" brand, which I will use across various topics in upcoming books. The concept is simple: to achieve your vision for any project, whether building a million-dollar business or writing a book, you must learn to work on it daily with set routines and processes, 365 days a year.

This doesn't mean that you have to dedicate hours per day to the project, but that it should be a part of your daily routine and focus.

Keep in mind too that enforced downtime is part of the process to create anything of value, from relationships to businesses.

This book adapts the "365 to Vision" concept to writing.

Although the lessons can be adapted by fiction novelists, poets, and playwrights (to name just a few), I focus on modern writers of the digital age—freelancers, bloggers, e-book writers, and those producing product copy.

I argue that 80% of successful writing is derived from two places:

- Direct author experience, from listening to everyday conversations to researching to daydreaming to scribbling/outlining in notebooks or apps.
- Daily productivity practices such as enforcing downtime between writing for ultimate creativity, optimizing time and routines, and the endless thirst to learn continuously.

The other 20% is through the actual process of writing and rewriting.

There are hundreds of books available about the elements of great writing that provide guidance on craft, style, and form. I still include thoughts about these elements in the initial two chapters, but recommend that you expand your understanding by referring to my favorite books throughout.

Above all, writing well takes passion. In that regard, it's the same as every other discipline where the *truly* successful experts stand out, from machinists to motorcycle racers to salesmen to carpenters.

Writing for me is an addiction. It has the dopamine hit of the most potent drug out there. Writing delivers the biological boost needed to positively live your days out the best you can with zero regrets.

I'm here to take you on a journey through what I've learned in my own path from writing poems at 14, to ghostwriting articles for CEOs that run million-dollar companies, to educating an audience after testing the latest Ducati or publishing content about entrepreneurship on *Forbes.*

The great writing teacher Don Murray says, "The most accurate definition of writing, I believe, is that it is the process of using language to discover meaning in experience and to communicate it. I believe this process can be described, understood and therefore learned."

I couldn't agree more. And I'm here to provide a few lessons about what I've learned over the past 25 years.

In writing *365 to Vision: Modern Writer's Guide, How to Produce More Quality Writing in Less Time*, my mission is to communicate the most useful lessons, share inspiring stories, and offer value for beginner and seasoned writers alike.

Enjoy.

CHAPTER 1

MODERN WRITER'S GUIDE TO CRAFT

Take 100 writers, from sci-fi novelists to poets, from playwrights to copywriters and bloggers and beyond, and each will provide a different take on the "craft" of writing.

The vast majority of these writers, I assure you, also struggle with their craft daily.

Merriam-Webster dictionary defines craft as the skill involved in planning, making, or executing. Most writers excel at one or two of these elements but rarely do they excel at all three.

For fiction writers, craft includes factors such as plot, characters, setting, foreshadowing, and irony, to name a *very* few. Creative writing professors offer lessons in these at every university with a writing program, and we're not going to spend our time here teaching those factors.

In this guide, we are exploring everyday ways to put the practice of your craft to work for you. I will share lessons learned from teachers and writers across genres, as well as those that became practice as I found ways to make life easier.

We look to Hunter S. Thompson for our first lesson in craft.

Though the subject matter of *Fear and Loathing in Las Vegas* is extreme, the content itself can be digested within a few hours.

The way Thompson's words flow demonstrates the work of a master craftsman—one who understood discipline, patience, and process. At his peak, from the 1960s through his death in 2005, Hunter practiced his craft 365 days a year whether by experiencing the events that exploded into scenes or actually behind his IBM Selectric Typewriter putting words to paper.

As most 21st Century writers know, especially those in the freelance realm, subjects vary drastically. To make that writing interesting, one must write from a voice of experience (even if that experience has nothing to do with the subject that they are writing about).

True craftspeople are at their writing 365 days a year. They have a vision they are working to achieve. Again, this takes patience, discipline, and a focus on the process of writing.

Back to Hunter S. quickly.

Here was a man whose addiction to mastering the writing craft, both behind the typewriter and in everyday life, eventually claimed his life. Early in his career, he took on the time-consuming tasks of rewriting the works of Fitzgerald word-for-word.

Did Hunter sound like Fitzgerald? No. But Hunter's storylines were easy to comprehend. His writing was enjoyable. He demonstrated the patience, discipline, and focus on the process of writing that makes one writer's work stand out against the backdrop of the others.

Maintaining these three elements is made much more manageable with a relentless passion for mastering craft. Though, as we'll discuss later, mastery may be too lofty an ideal; it is the ongoing attempts at mastery that drive a deeper understanding of words and how to communicate them clearly.

Following are some thoughts of craft for the 21st Century writer that I have learned from the best writers dead and alive, and my own relentless studies.

Scribbles and Outlines

I'm a sucker for productivity. Is there anything better than accomplishing the highest quality work done in the least amount of time? It is important to note though that the actual "working" part of writing begins long before putting pen to paper (or fingers to keyboard, as the case may be).

I'm talking about scribbles, which are notes scribbled down no matter where I am. I physically write these thoughts down, though others use apps.

Most of my scribbles emerge while doing things beyond the scope or thought of writing: Riding motorcycles at triple-digit speeds, taking a bath, hiking in the woods, flirting with my wife. I carry a Moleskine tablet everywhere (the cheap Cahier ones that cost 10 bucks for a three-pack) to jot these thoughts down.

When thoughts I may want to explore later surface, I make bullets in my tablet. Some are sloppy single-liners; others are four pages of thoughts. I may have 100 ideas for a chapter or story scribbled out and only a couple make it into any finalized piece of work.

Regardless, this process of scribbling gets thoughts down on paper.

These scribbles may turn into an outline for whatever I'm working on (not the first draft, but an outline).

Often, these are the thoughts I want to discover and exploit. Those thoughts transition into subtopics I want to explore, then to ideas about the target audience I want to reach. Some scribbles are a list of headlines for a piece I'm thinking about or a draft I have written already.

Sometimes these scribbles are magical. Other times they are pure garbage.

I've carried some sort of tablet around with me since the late 1990s. I don't understand the muse or science-based principles, but I do understand that writing is above all a process that happens, in some way, every day. Sometimes an idea needs a decade or two to percolate in the mind. And when it's time for that thought to be explored, the energy from those original scribbles flows back like a scene in a movie you've watched a few times before.

Every few months, I spend a day revisiting my scribble tablets from years past looking for ideas that fizzled out then, but are useful now.

Writers are at it 365 days a year, until they reach that vision of discovery in their head. Sometimes it takes a decade or three.

Screw Notifications

Every writer—even the most disciplined—struggles at times with productivity and time management. We'll take a more granular look into this in Chapter 4, but one crucial element needs your attention now.

The repetition of your practice, every hour of every day, helps things stick. This is precisely why I've mentioned—and will continue to mention—patience, discipline, and the process of writing as the three elements that make great writers stand out among their peers, over and over again.

We've grown accustomed to allowing interruptions to the repetitive, healthy practices that build our craft. Ping! Buzz! Beep! I'm talking about email, text, and social media notifications. We are consumed by daily hits of dopamine from that Facebook like or retweet or text message.

Yet one little disturbance can kill the most amazing flow of writing. Focus is imperative to free thought, whether in the first or final draft. Why do we do this to ourselves?

Take all notifications and silence them.

I still fall victim to these productivity killers, though now it happens a few times a month rather than a few times a day.

Distractions displace your flowing words with the tedium of a return email or a response to a Facebook message. This immediate feedback loop supplies dopamine hits equal to a heroin fix for an addict.

Make those distractions nonexistent by having the discipline to tune out.

Timothy Leary asked people of the mid-1960s to, "Turn on, tune in, drop out." I'm asking you to turn off, tune out, and drop into your focus so you can create writing that truly stands out.

I've also learned to completely shut off my computer's WiFi, a tactic I picked up from Tim Ferriss, author of *The 4-Hour Workweek*. This simple practice prevents the distracted mind from answering anything that's not in the mindset of your focus.

For those who cannot write without feedback due to the psychological need for an immediate answer, try killing Wifi on your computer and phone but keeping a Google Home, Alexa Echo, or Siri device nearby. A voice assistant can answer the stupid questions that muddy up your thought process and "force" you to tune into the internet.

Sometimes you need immediate answers to questions that will nag you. You may legitimately need questions answered; I know I do during the editing process. I literally just asked Alexa, "What was the name of Google's talking device?" to finish the above edit.

My computer's WiFi is currently off.

I keep an Amazon Echo Dot next to my desk for quick research. (I have an Echo Show, as well, but it doesn't belong in the office where it can quickly jack your focus due to the video factor.)

Kill notifications during the act of writing. Your words and subsequent readers will thank you.

Go Landscaping, Line by Line

I took an online class in 2016 with Charles Euchner, author of *The Elements of Writing*.

I had already learned much of the information in other books on writing, as many repeat the same messages about clearing clutter and focusing on the target audience.

These books also typically discuss the mindset before, during, and after writing. But not so much about the page you're writing on.

Enter Euchner.

He has helped ease the process of writing through two simple tactics.

First, he advises altering the page setup of your document—whether in Google Docs (which I use) or in Microsoft Word—in landscape mode instead of the standard portrait layout.

This makes the document wider, and sentences span further across the page.

Next, Euchner recommends that you complete the first few drafts sentence-by-sentence.

Don't create paragraphs until you complete your first rounds of edits.

The single-line sentences keep the mind fresh, and they'll help corral thoughts as you begin editing.

The spacing between sentences opens up space for mental clarity.

This tactic forces you to think short for every sentence (much like a Tweet in 280 characters) so you can embrace concise writing.

This spacing technique also helps you establish a much-needed rhythm between long and short sentences. Some need more length to help solidify a previous thought or introduce the next thought, and some are shorter to communicate a point quicker.

I adhere to these Euchner tips about 80 percent of my writing time. The exception is when I'm creating a more creative "spew" draft. I grew up on Kerouac and practiced spontaneous prose while working drafts.

But after those drafts are complete, I truly get to a first draft by cutting out half of the BS and arranging my work line-by-line.

Try it. Set your Word or Google Docs page to a landscape mode and write your first few drafts sentence-by-sentence.

This simple practice helps you focus, gain clarity, and quickly recognize what doesn't belong.

Or does.

You now got some insights into scribbling, outlining, and setting up a draft's page for clear thinking.

They are a few vital steps on craft.

If you take anything away from this chapter, I hope it is this: scribbling, outlining, and setting up your draft for maximum clarity will supercharge your writing process.

Now it's time to spew.

Spew When Drunk, Edit When Sober

Write drunk. Edit sober.

Four words. Two complete thoughts, each separated in this example in much the same way as the shortest sentence in the bible: "Jesus wept."

Papa Hemingway didn't actually say, "Write drunk, edit sober." But many have attributed it to him due to the nature of his personal character.

Papa drank. And drank. And drank.

But he also wrote. And wrote. And wrote. (Some argue he never wrote while drunk.)

Modern studies show that all that boozing went to his head. Indeed, it did in the most literal sense on July 2, 1961, in Ketchum, Idaho.

I'm not here to refute his boozing or popularize it. But there is a lesson in understanding your moments of creativity when at the keyboard.

Whatever your outlet, create a mood to get words flowing in the most natural way possible. Zero editing, zero looking back.

When you return during later drafts with a clear mind, the magic continues to happen.

Think of these creative let-go drafts as spew drafts. It's not actually a complete first draft just yet, but a spew draft.

And, most importantly, have fun with them.

For me, this is the most enjoyable part of the writing process. I get away from it all during my spew drafting. For example, writing this book took me well into the 3 a.m. slots many Thursday mornings during the COVID-19 quarantine. That escape was something I needed at the time.

First, you must get to the writing and puke those words onto a page.

Everyone has their "drunk" moments when words flow. For some, the process begins with meditation. For others, it's an early morning hike in the woods. For others still, it's sex.

You get the point.

Whatever works to find those creative moments, do it. Stick with what produces the best results.

What works for me when actually at the keyboard completing the first spew? Sipping homemade red wine and listening to music in my "Reality Room," a 25- x 25-foot open space above the garage, detached from the house, overlooking the woods, while my wife and son, Enzo, are sleeping.

It is a combination that works wonders. It puts me into that focus-drunk place most conducive to writing freely, especially when I begin with some head-clearing activities.

This doesn't always work, though. At times, I may need a triple-digit motorcycle ride around the mountains to get my mind totally off of writing before I can even begin to think about typing a word. Other times, sitting on one of the vintage white iron chairs on my porch and reviewing bullet points from one of my Moleskine tablets does the trick.

You know your process. Embrace it, regardless of how weird or normal it may seem.

Whatever it takes, spew, spew, spew. Get it all out with zero regards for edits or attribution to whatever sources you need to establish trust from the reader. Allow yourself to just go with it - don't correct spellings, worry about grammatical mistakes, or facts. Just let the words flow.

The next step is to walk away. Let that draft sit and "sleep on it."

The mind does amazing things when you let a piece of work go cold, then return to it with a fresh and hot mind. It gets you away from the conscious thought of what you're writing and allows your subconscious to put the pieces together.

Chris Bailey sums up this process of letting the subconscious mind get to work in a book every writer should read: *Hyperfocus*. He says, "Simple decisions are best made using cold, hard logic.

"This way, we can work through the incremental steps that lead to an answer. But the same isn't true for complex decisions, ones that require more creativity in meshing together a web of interconnected ideas. These decisions can be impossible to work through with logic and reason alone. That's why we need to tap into the proven power of our subconscious mind."

A refreshed look that makes all the difference. That first step of a writer's craft is to simply get the words out of your head. Worry about drafting and editing later.

Spew, spew, spew.

Often, the words will come out in long paragraphs of jumbled shit.

No worries. Now it's time for a first draft—the one where your words began to make sense.

First Draft Post-Spew Outline, with Organization in Mind

Drafting is where your writing becomes coherent. A serious first draft takes your spew draft and creates a logical readable story from it.

The 80/20 rule—making sure 20 percent of your efforts achieve 80 percent of the result—surfaces quickly when you begin drafting. Your first draft may reflect 80 percent of your effort having gone into 20 percent of the ideas that need to be explained. Now, you can cut useless ideas and words aggressively.

Don't be afraid of this process; it's only your first *real* draft. Think about your first moments at anything—driving a car, romanticizing someone, learning to play a song, whatever. Most would likely never repeat what happened first.

The same thought process goes for your first round of edits. I use a simple 4-part outline formula for creating a first draft based on my "spew" draft:

- Think 80/20 and cut what is useless.
- Rewrite.
- Repeat the above two points after "sleeping on it."
- Polish a first draft.

When writing a blog, I'll sometimes begin with 2,500 words from a spew draft. I'll cut that to 1,800 words in a first draft, rewrite, and cut again. Typically, just half the words remain.

Rewrite and restructure your first draft until it says everything you want to say in the most coherent way.

I don't necessarily do first, second, third, fourth, or however many drafts are needed to accomplish my goals. Sometimes it takes a single draft with 50 edits. Other times it requires 10 drafts with 500 edits. Do what is needed, but make sure drafting is in play. It's worth every second of effort, and your readers will thank you.

Then, walk away again. Your mind will be fresh and you will better be able to get your message across when you return to get organized.

Even if your first working draft is just 1,000 words, it pays to organize your writing. Organized writing equates to organized thoughts.

Always organize with your end goals in mind, asking the following:

- What do I want to achieve here?
- What is my overall mission with this blog, chapter, etc.?
- Why would I waste time writing if there was no ending in mind?
- Are my thoughts organized so the reader actually gets the meaning?
- Should I scrap this section, or rewrite it, or place it somewhere different?
- Again, is this actually worth my time?

As for the actual editing process of a first draft, some prefer to start at the beginning and go from there. Others focus on editing the beginning and ending before the middle, and others still vice versa. Find what works for you. Experiment with both back-to-back, and find your way.

Walk Away. Again.

Practicing your craft each day does not mean relentlessly writing and editing hour after hour, day after day, ad nauseum. If you stay at it too long, fogginess surfaces.

You can continue writing a spew draft until your head explodes, because that's what that process is all about. A bit of fogginess is okay.

During drafting, though, fogginess kills creativity and productivity. This is when it's time to take a break - even if your ego won't let you. When you complete that one draft you're proud of but starting to struggle with words, kill your ego and flee. Make a habit of this.

Depending on the size of the piece, this walking away process may take a few hours, days, weeks, months, or even years. I've been away from the final draft of my debut fiction novel for nearly 10 years. Yes, a decade. I worked on another three drafts that have grown to 250,000 words and shrunk to 125,000 words, but I'm simply not ready to finish that book.

That novel is for my relaxation. It is not work that needs finishing so I can help create value for other writers in the 21st Century.

But it is there, in the back of my head, 365 days a year. It is there waiting until that vision happens.

As for freelancers who actually pay the bills with the words they produce, deadlines matter. Make the best of your time between drafts to get energetic, discover what you want to say, and rewrite until your words communicate with ease.

If you have a piece of content due in two weeks, outline now and spew some words, then create a first draft. Walk away, organize, and think.

Then...

Write - and Rewrite. And Rewrite again

All right, so you have your few drafts down.

Time to rewrite.

Who said writing was easy?

In *Writing to Learn*, William Zinsser says, "Only by repeated applications of the process—writing and rewriting and pruning and shaping—can we hammer out clear and simple product."

This is a true artist's position on writing; one who also understands that writing takes (yes, I'll say it again) patience, discipline, and a focus on the process.

Words may arrive easily for some, and slowly for others. But the only words that stick, and do the duty of educating and entertaining (with a mission of doing both at the same time),survive rewriting.

The goal is to outline, spew some words, and begin drafting. Writing is underway 365 days a year until you reach your vision - never forget that. Then rewrite, rewrite, and rewrite.

Repeat the process as many times as necessary until things are clear.

Most writers new to the 365 to Vison discipline fall deeply for their first drafts, thinking all is perfect.

I was once a culprit. After re-reading my older stories, many as old as floppy discs themselves, I realized everything could be cut. Two-hundred and fifty words became 25. Chapters became bullet points within other chapters.

This chapter was once over 10,000 words. After four rewrites, it was cut in half.

This cutting is all part of the rewriting process. Don't skimp here. Think like a reader. Read passages aloud and ask yourself if the reader can understand what you're saying in the clearest way.

Write. Rewrite. And rewrite again as many times as necessary to achieve your mission.

Always use less words. And always keep the intended audience in mind.

Hard Copy for Final Edits

People read differently on print versus the screen, which is why I rely on hard copies for my final edits.

When you are 100 percent satisfied with your draft, print it out for editing.

This is when I discover flow issues, cluttered thoughts, and repetitions.

For example, I was extremely happy with my "final" screen draft for this book. Upon printing it out, I logged another seven hours of marking up and implementing each edit.

Remember that if you have used Euchner's landscape mode for drafting, you need to switch your document to portrait mode before printing. If not, you'll be reading papers horizontally (which drives me crazy).

Use a Framework

You know to keep your work clear and simple, but sometimes the writing doesn't flow and sounds cluttered.

Try creating a framework of main ideas and backfilling them. This is something you can learn through reading the best of the best in other disciplines besides writing.

In the past, I would imagine myself as a reader and create a list of bullet points they may see as a problem. I would then follow up by proposing multiple solutions to those problems.

This worked, but it took time. Then I discovered Donald Miller's book *Building a StoryBrand,* a must-read for those involved in digital marketing, but also incredibly valuable for modern writers who want to communicate in a clear and concise way.

Building a Storybrand offers multiple tactics for overcoming issues by focusing on building a story around the target reader.

One small section around creating a "one-liner" (which is not actually one line but a full thought) has helped me create a framework for writing any type of content. It simplifies the message and provides endless clarity.

The framework is a roadmap with four components:

1. The Character
2. The Problem
3. The Plan
4. The Success

For each piece of writing, you supply answers to these components and create a one-liner (which, again, doesn't exactly have to be one line, but you get the point).
An example would be:

1. The Character: motorcyclist passionate about the freedom of riding, but afraid of crashing.
2. The Problem: Can't overcome mental fear.
3. The Plan: Remove fear through teaching underlying principles of motorcycle safety, both psychological and physical.
4. The Success: A renewed passion for riding and calmness in life.

The one-liner above would read: "We help those passionate about motorcycles overcome the mental fear of motorcycling through teaching proven principles—both psychological and physical—that create a safer and more confident rider, renewing their passion for riding. This reduced anxiety and greater relaxation allows for additional time to spend on other important things, like family and work."

These one-liners have helped me create a framework for any type of written content, from product copy to service pages to FAQs to daily blogging for clients, and chapters for books.

Talk It Out

Sometimes we know deep down what we want to say, but can't get the message across with clarity and simplicity. This is where talking it out does wonders (even when talking to yourself).

Others that you trust (and even those you do not trust) can provide you with serious energy to get the flow of your words just right.

Find a competent and clear-minded person for a discussion. They don't have to be experts on the subject; just make sure they are capable of listening and providing a no-BS answer to what you're trying to figure out in your head.

Sometimes, those with zero subject matter knowledge can provide the best responses.

If I created copy for a website that targeted small businesses with no clue as to how SEO works, for example, I wouldn't want to talk it out with an SEO expert. I wouldn't turn to the readers and contributors at a publication I write for, *Search Engine Journal*, even though they are great people and a part of my community.

Rather, I'd target a small business owner who had experienced success in building a digital presence. This person has a grasp on the process, whether the work was outsourced or brought in-house, but is far from an expert. That person would help me simplify things, and provide clarity for the target reader.

Having another competent human's input is helpful. But many writers I know are introverts (including myself, until a few years ago).

Talking it out doesn't necessarily mean talking to someone else. You can talk it out with yourself, without feeling crazy about it. It's part of a writer's life.

Write Whatever Works First

There should be no hierarchy or priority in spew or draft modes. If you have the energy for an intro, write it.

Subtopics? Write them. Title? Conclusion? Write it.

Whatever works. All will come together smoothly and in a more organized fashion during the equally (and sometimes more important) editing stages.

Your Title Needs as Much Thought as Your Draft

This is a tip that most books on writing emphasized especially resources on writing digital content.

Put as much time into crafting your titles as you do the articles.

The best headlines:

- Create curiosity
- Ask questions
- Use numbers (odd numbers psychologically get more clicks—more on that below)
- Create a sense of urgency
- Show "how to" do something
- Establish credibility
- Explain benefits of a product or service
- Start a conversation in the reader's head
- Explain the "WHY" of your brand (read Simon Sinek)

Don't think that these have to be super creative. Sometimes titles are so creative, they create confusion. For example, imagine reading the headline "Pop Art is Unequivocally Brash Nowadays - Start Dissecting Cubism." Would this appeal to you, even if you were super familiar with both art movements?

You can have the best piece of content in the world, but if the title is not engaging not many people will notice. Genius copywriters like Ray Edwards say that you have a mere two seconds to garner attention with your headline.

First, for search engine optimization (SEO) purposes that will help your piece get found (something that I'll discuss in Chapter 6), you must keep that title around 60 characters (not 60 words). This helps get your message across before search engines truncate the title.

Also, according to the well-respected Backlinko[3], two things that are statistically said to attract attention from a psychological stance within titles are:

- Brackets or parentheses
- Odd numbers

Put the effort into creating headlines that work.

And just as the craft of writing drafts says walk away, do the same for those headlines. Treat them like articles/books in and of themselves in the way you practice writing.

---

3 https://backlinko.com/hub/seo/organic-ctr

Attention-Grabbing Intro

While the title grabs attention to get the reader to your page, the first paragraph of any piece—from a blog to a chapter to a technical article—can keep them there.

Use the same principle as the title.

Entertain. Piss off. Create curiosity.

Do whatever it takes to engage the reader with true authenticity. Don't be fake. Keep readers engaged by explaining what's in it for them in the clearest way.

Stuck with Flow? Think About How Press Releases Are Written

I've received and written press releases for businesses and clients for over two decades.

Sometimes when I write, I use a simple format borrowed from the book *Free PR: How to Get Chased by the Press Without Hiring a PR Firm* by the best-selling author and former COO at 1-800-GOT-JUNK?, Cameron Harold, and coauthor Adrian Salamunovic.

I rely on this format when I find that a piece of content (blog, chapter, etc.) lacks flow or begs for restructuring:

- Catchy headline
- Catchy lead paragraph
- Expose a problem
- Show how your product/service can solve that problem

- Provide hard data or facts
- Quote someone high within the company (CEO, CMO, Founder)
- Quote a customer or influencer
- Provide a call-to-action (absolutely vital for online service and product pages, and blogs)

Try it. The simple format works. And it'll amp up your craft as a writer.

Know Your Audience

To write effectively, you must understand the target audience. You'll explain things much differently to an audience nearing retirement versus a teenager.

If you're a freelancer, agency/company leaders will likely provide you this information.

This is where marketing materials need to be shared and CEOs need to engage the blogger or agency. Also, sometimes there are various target audiences due to where a prospect is within the sales funnel, and it is a company or marketing leader's duty to explain this.

Writers, especially freelance writers who work with various companies, should be in constant conversation with the sales team, which is typically closest to the client and understands the client's needs and questions. This will help you expand on topics and provide more value to readers.

Extended Thoughts on Craft - The Mechanics of Writing

Let's get granular about the mechanics of writing.

These quick tips can help you level up in your process and produce more serious results.

Build Words Around Questions

- Always ask what's the problem and how can I clearly provide a solution to that problem.
- As importantly, ask if readers will care? This will help keep your voice trustworthy and authoritative.

Appeal to All Senses

- Don't just appeal to sight, as much writing does. Also appeal to other senses, such as smell, sound, touch, and taste.
- Try to appeal to all five senses in every piece of content you create. If you're writing an editorial about the latest destructive city riot, discuss not only the sights, but the smell such as plastic burning within the air; the sound such as a child's voice amid adult voices; the touch such as broken glass underneath your shoes; and the taste such as sulfur on the tongue.

Think Like a Camera

- When writing, think like a camera: provide input from aerial views, up close, in the middle of it all, and behind the scenes.
- Let your audience experience the moment, and not just read about it.

Split Longer Projects Into Shorter Tasks

With a blog, for example, write all headlines first and fill in each portion. This works if you're writing a 2,500-word piece on the craft of writing, or a 750-piece for a client discussing technical aspects of a product.

Writing a 12-chapter book? Treat each chapter as its own book. Always remember to connect all chapters during the final revisions.

Always Keep the End in Mind

Where are you going? Always have an ending in mind as you write. This helps keep focus sharp and assists in the ultimate goal of all writing – the conversation. And for most blog writing, a conversion.

Check and Recheck

Check, and recheck, spelling and grammar. Misspell a name and the article immediately loses credibility.

Craft with sloppy grammar and the article loses credibility.

Read Passages Backward

This is for grammar. Read the entire piece backward, starting from the last paragraph to the top. You'll quickly find errors because your mind won't be in flow or organizational mode.

Credibility Matters

Credibility is to your brand what keywords are to SEO.

Without credibility, you lose any chance to capture the audience's attention. You are disqualified before you're even out of the gate. The situation worsens if you spread misinformation, even unintentionally. Take the time required for thorough research and fact-checking.

Busy and want to save time to put more energy into writing (80/20 thinking)? Outsource the fact-checking and research to a virtual assistant.

Try Writing in Longhand

When I was spewing and drafting early on in the process of writing this book, I read off scribble tablet notes I had taken earlier while flying over the Atlantic Ocean en route to a motorcycle launch in Valencia, Spain.

Traveling on planes, trains, and Ubers provides optimal time and space for thinking and using longhand. Plus, especially while flying, it keeps your mind off annoying passengers (snore much?). Also, try longhand writing for meeting notes and, of course, in the margins of paperback or hardcover books.

Try it, and revisit your scribble tablets religiously throughout the entire editorial process.

Journalism Thoughts

I trained as a journalist. Not with Harvard or Columbia, mind you, but at a community college, along with five years in the proverbial trenches, writing daily under deadline.

I dedicate Chapter 5 to this, but for this chapter on writing craft, understand the 5 Ws and How.

Think like a journalist; ask *and answer* the who, what, when, where, why, and, most importantly, how.

And remember - never cram all these five Ws and how into one paragraph. Not only will this present clutter to the reader, but search engines can see this as spammy and keyword stuffed.

Write so the flow is natural.

Create 110% Original Content

Yes, 110 percent. In theory, anything over 100 percent is impossible, but using 110 stresses that writers should strive for complete originality.

I'm sure at some point you've read numerous articles on the same subject and gotten lost in how similar they are. We see this often in hot topics. It happens much in the digital marketing world as writers trip over one another to get their opinions heard.

Some are just trying to pump out endless blogs or pages in hopes of making a dent in the search results, as well. But one original article that delivers originality will overcome 100 worthless ones.

Like poor grammar or spelling, there is no mercy for plagiarism.

Plagiarism—even the most minimal version of it—will immediately sever the relationship and can result in much public embarrassment.

Content Lacks Fluff

All writing efforts should support the overall mission of TAR: Trust, Authority, and Respect.

Kill the fluff and sales-forward or "me, me, me" copy. Focus on writing content built to establish TAR.

Never overuse adjectives or adverbs. Most are useless, though some may be a *major* help. Again I'll refer you back to the true talent of no fluff; read Hemingway, the master of simplicity.

Be Remarkable

Stand out. Be original. Don't write like your competitors.

Read Seth Godin's *Purple Cow: Transform Your Business by Being Remarkable*. The text can be read in under two hours and will teach you everything you need to know about being remarkable.

Quick Craft Thoughts

Much was discussed here on craft, so let's recap and provide some other quick points:

- During your first post-spew edit, cut out anything useless. Adjectives, adverbs, crappy passages, or stuff that appears out of place.
- Use the paid version of Grammarly. It's genius. Always have a grammar book handy. Two of my favorites are *The best punctuation book, period.* by June Casagrande, and *The Only Grammar Book You'll Ever Need* by Susan Thurman.
- Use subject-matter experts for things you question or don't know. Cite those credible experts in your works.
- Read out loud. You'll be able to find mistakes quickly, from grammar to voice. Start from the top and strengthen anything that feels or sounds weak.
- Read passages backward: This is for grammar. Read the entire piece backward, starting from the last paragraph to the top. You'll quickly find errors because your mind won't be in flow or organizational mode.
- Have a peer review your work, whether a subject matter expert or not. Never submit to an editor or publisher without another having another set of eyes on the writing.
- Walk away and edit again. Let your subconscious go to work.

Remember, perfectionism is just another form of procrastination. Get your writing out and let the readers decide its merit. And if they find mistakes, live up to them; we're human and fallible.

Craft is vital, as is a strong editorial process.

Onwards, as my favorite CEO Howard Schultz says, to some thoughts on form.

Chapter 2

Modern Writer's Guide to Form

For those who study poetry, the form versus function debate never ends.

Here's one of my favorite opening lines from Charles Bukowski, who many don't rate as a true "poet." His poem "splash" begins:

> the illusion is that you are simply
> reading this poem.
> the reality is that this is
> more than a
> poem.

What did you pay attention to? The lines or the meaning?

Form refers to the positioning of lines (e.g.: five stanzas of four lines), along with rhyme and meter schemes. Function refers to elements such as meaning and theme.

Does form follow function, or does function follow form?

For writers besides poets, this may mean absolute shit in the purest form of these two words combined: absolute shit.

But it matters—especially for nonfiction writers who make their living by writing.

For nonfiction writers, proper form is non-negotiable. It allows you to communicate your message to the reader in the strongest possible way. Form is much easier to adhere to as a nonfiction writer versus a poet.

Most writers, regardless of discipline, agree on the following thoughts on form. None of these are 100% original thoughts; each is derived from the works and teachings of the best writers and writing teachers worldwide, past, and present.

We'll begin with some major issues in regards to form, and follow up with short and snappy solutions. Once implemented into the 365 to Vision writer lifestyle, your words will have more of an impact on not only the reader, but on you as a writer.

Studying form daily helps me stay true to my focus on patience, discipline, and the process of writing, again three elements that help writers stand out amongst the noise.

Simplicity and Clarity: The Core of Good Writing

Leonardo da Vinci says it perfectly: "Simplicity is the ultimate sophistication."

When a reader first encounters a piece of writing, simplicity and clarity must trump all. If a grade-schooler can't understand, don't expect the ideas to come across clear and simple. (There's a reason it is best practice to write to an eighth-grade level or lower for the web.)

Simplicity to ease the task of unraveling the concepts behind complex content begins with a clean flow of sentences.

Did you have to return to that sentence to understand it? That line was challenging, and needs a rewrite: A clean sentence easily unravels complex concepts.

Following the flow, a writer should avoid topic-specific jargon and complex words unless writing for a specific audience within a niche—say, a medical journal for doctors or scientists.

Sometimes you are forced to write about a complex topic.

This happens often when I write about digital marketing for a publication like *Forbes*. Yes, I must get into some technical jargon. But I must also pay my due diligence and explain that jargon in the simplest form.

For example, what if you had to write about using ethnographic research to improve a website's user experience (something I was tasked to complete in 2016)?

First, you would immediately define the terms; ethnographic derives from ethnography, the study of people and cultures. "Ethnographic research," then, is the study of businesspeople in their natural environments, and the subsequent use of the data produced within research.

The more complex a subject, the more complex the jargon. The mission is to use super simple language to describe exactly what that jargon means. Writers must educate with ease, something every reader craves in a world of constant disruptions.

One author that comes to mind is Anthony William, known as the "Medical Medium." His books are thick and get into very tough medical talk.

Take his book *Liver Rescue*, for example. The book discusses complex medical issues that are typically reserved for doctors and health experts, but he makes the content digestible for those who don't study medicine or health.

Thanks to his simple style of writing, readers like me—those like countless others with minimal medical knowledge who want to improve their own health—can understand William with ease.

His simple language allows a person as far removed from medical thinking as I am to grasp his important lessons and guidance about strengthening a liver for optimal health.

Had he filled the book with complex medical terms and jargon, most non-medical types would quickly lose interest. His important teachings would fail to reach their intended audience.

Albert Einstein said, "I speak to everyone in the same way, whether he is the garbage man or the president of the university."

That is *exactly* how to get your message across clearly and concisely.

Active vs Passive Voice

An active voice delivers a clearer message than the passive voice.

The difference is simple.

When an active voice is used, the subject performs the action. With passive voice, the action is received by the subject.

A quick example:

- **Active:** Danny wrote the blog.
- **Passive:** The blog was written by Danny.

The active voice is much simpler to understand and is vital when writing about a complex subject. Though the passive voice is needed sometimes to emphasize action over the actor (you are not allowed to drive after too many drinks) or to emphasize strong words at the end of a sentence, stick with the active voice wherever possible.

Active voice delivers a clear message. It is quick and concise. While writing in the active voice, also remember to keep sentences short and punchy. Shorter sentences not only help produce clearer messages but also read better on mobile devices, something digital writers must always keep top of mind.

Yes, you'll use longer sentences to carry readers through situations that demand deeper energy. But for the most part, writing short works better.

Energetic Pose with Reader Involved

Readers can immediately recognize when a writer is bored by their own words. If not consciously, then certainly unconsciously.

The best way to battle this? Write with energy, allowing the prose to reflect exactly how excited you are about a subject. The more complex the content, the more energy you must display.

A simple way to create energy around a complex topic is to use anecdotes that people can easily relate to (think of current events or stories with broad appeal).

Jocko Willink does this well in *Extreme Ownership: How U.S. Navy SEALs Lead and Win*.

I'm not a military buff, but the stories exuded so much energy that I couldn't put the book down. I finished it within two sittings and took away hundreds of lessons due to the energetic quality of the prose.

Anecdotes of SEALs triumphing in Ramadi raised the energy, and within those were embedded the complex leadership skills that otherwise may have been difficult to digest. Willinik was able to explain these skills in simpler terms, now that his war anecdotes had seized your attention.

And don't forget some straightforward analogies. Back to Anthony William who, in his book *Medical Medium: Secrets Behind Chronic and Mystery Illness and How to Finally Heal*, wrote, "Your heart serves as the compass for your actions, guiding you to do the right thing when your soul becomes lost."

That's memorable, and it brings such clarity to a complex subject.

Check Google Trends and Quora to inform your keyword research for high-volume terms when creating your anecdotes. This little bit of research can help you stumble onto a topic you wouldn't have thought of otherwise.

Consistent with the Delivery of Voice and Style

Give your writing a consistent voice. Don't be funny one paragraph or chapter, satirical the next, and serious in between. Use the same voice and style for each piece of writing, whether a novel, article, blog, or newsletter.

In regards to style, many like Associated Press (AP), some prefer the American Psychology Association (APA), and others still swear by the Chicago Manual of Style. Again, whatever you choose, stick with it.

Most copy on the web is written in AP styling, which is what newspapers and most magazines use. I use AP style, except for those debatable Oxford commas (that I now embrace after 15 years of despising them). Keep the *AP Stylebook* PDF or, better yet, the book version handy so you can refer to it as needed.

Another great reference book that covers AP and other styles like APA is *The best punctuation book, period.* by June Casagrande. This book should always be at arm's length.

Embrace Short Paragraphs

Keep paragraphs short, unless you have a list of bullet points. This creates "air" around your sentences, and the words are more pleasing to the eye.

Don't be afraid of single-sentence paragraphs; they make a point stand out.

The longer the paragraph, the faster a reader will lose interest. Long paragraphs look complicated to the mind on a PC or Mac—and these complications increase 100-fold for audiences reading on mobile.

Short paragraphs allow the mind to breathe. Use them often. Space between paragraphs psychologically takes less energy to read, saving that prospect's energy for understanding what you're communicating.

The Sharp Bullets on Form

Hundreds of books exist on form, and a lot of serious writers have read them all.

But many haven't.

To keep things simple and valuable for each, I'll finish with some simple bullets. I have this list on a "splash" sheet in my Google Drive and keep it open in a tab during my final editing stages. It reminds me of the basics on form that are too easy to forget.

Also, some of the repetition here is intentional:

- The strongest words should begin and end a sentence, and the strongest sentences should be placed at the end and beginning of a paragraph. This helps keep the slower material in the middle of a sentence, and the most important thoughts before the reader.
- Kill clutter. Strip all useless words. Get sentences into their simplest form.
- Beware excess adverbs and adjectives. If the verb or noun can't perform the explanation, it isn't strong enough.
- Always use active verbs so you have an active voice. Without active verbs, the mind shifts and wanders. You lose the audience... and possible sales of your work.
- Use simple language. Unless you're writing for a specific audience that uses highly technical terms, keep jargon out of your writing. If you're forced to use jargon, explain it.
- Use the active voice. Can I emphasize this enough? Harry met Sally. The man walked the dog. The blogger wrote the blog. Verbs should show action. Work hard to keep them active. Use passive voice for rhythm and to alter flow for rhythm.

- Use proper grammar. Read *The Elements of Style* by Strunk and White. Use Grammarly (as I mentioned in Chapter 1, the paid version is worth its editing weight in gold).
- Avoid clichés like the plague. You feel that one. Clichés dilute writing. Don't get caught between a rock and a hard place by using clichés. From sea to shining sea and all four corners of the earth, your blog writing will have readers thinking they got the short end of the stick. Cat got your tongue? Good. Don't use clichés.
- Most sentences (like this one) are created in a "right-branching" method, meaning the subject and verb of the main clause occur early, followed by supporting elements. But Roy Peter Clark says that we should create some instances of the periodic sentence, which allows you to "build and build to a verb or a main clause near the end." He uses the popular song lyrics "Over the river and through the woods to Grandmother's house we go," which delivers a stronger effect than, "We go to grandmother's house, over the river and through the woods."
- Establish rhythm with long and short sentences. When writing, mix long and short sentences to establish a rhythm and control the pace. Think of mixing the short and snappy active style of Hemingway with the long and sometimes passive style of Faulk-

ner. Writing needs rhythm. Its shows that the author cares not only about pumping out content, but also entertaining the reader.

- Let punctuation help control the pace. Besides long and short sentences, punctuation informs the pace. And rather quickly. Think about it; there are loads of ways to speed up or slow down a sentence.
- Watch your "ings." Sometimes they are needed for slowing the flow or making a point, but they can weaken verbs and actions.
- Use dialogue to show action when using a direct quote from a person or publication. The gnarlier the quote, the more it'll propel the reader excitedly through the story. Bret Easton Ellis masters this. Read *Lunar Park* and you'll understand. And quickly.
- Use a consistent voice. Every author has his or her unique voice. If they don't, with patience, discipline and a steady flow of writing, 365 days a year, that voice will arrive. Make sure that voice is the same across every blog. Over the past 20 years, I've ghostwritten hundreds of articles for CEOs and entrepreneurs and developed a unique voice for each one. Since departing ways with some, a few have used different ghostwriters, which is evident in the lack of consistent voice. Work hard to develop your voice... and work harder to keep that

voice consistent across every piece of writing.

- Use consistent themes within each piece of writing. Themes reinforce the storytelling behind the copy, from blogs to books. Themes provide entertainment for readers, allowing them to look forward to something more (even if on a subconscious level).
- Use a consistent style. Keep the proper tense (first, second, or third) throughout, although some (especially longer) pieces will benefit by switching between tenses.
- Become obsessed about clarity of voice and topic. Clean writing reflects a clear mindset, something people need. Keep all writing free of clutter. Keep it simple. Get straight to what you're saying. If you're stuck with clarity of voice and topic, think about the theme. Revisit the main theme of your article, and rewrite it as one short sentence. This will help you achieve clarity. This practice is also something that helps as a reminder during the post-spew drafts of longer books. I start new chapters in new documents and place that simple theme at the top of every document. This book's theme is "Guidebook for modern writers, educating on process to productivity through storytelling."

Can I Repeat It One More Time?

Edit. Then edit again, and yet again. And again, if necessary.

After two decades of writing, I cut more "noise" out of final drafts than ever before, always keeping the thoughts on form fresh in my mind.

This noise is only removed through ruthless editing. Look out for useless words, or any ideas that don't simply explain the message.

Simplify for clarity. Your readers will thank you.

During editing, read things out loud; you'll find useless material, and quickly. And never forget to take time to walk away; especially before the final draft. I find my "final" draft is typically two-to-three drafts away, once I walk away and let my mind subconsciously connect the dots.

I'm far from a scientist or psychologist, but the walking away process works. And so does sticking with a strict routine, which we'll explore next.

Chapter 3

Modern Writer's Guide to Routines

Remember grade and middle school?

I don't.

Only a few vague memories remain, rehashed from a few photos and classmates' stories from the early 1990s, when smartphones didn't capture thousands of memories daily.

An automobile accident at 14 washed out most of my youth. Luckily, I had by then grown enough to have a rod inserted into my broken femur versus being plunged into a body cast.

That was 1994, the summer before those anxiety-filled first days of high school. That titanium rod streamlined the typical six-month recovery into two months, but it required a strict routine.

I bent my knee millimeters at a time through daily rehab. I kept my mind active by practicing guitar and transcribing music by ear, from Hendrix to Zeppelin to Nirvana to Metallica to Wes Montgomery.

My musical tastes were everywhere then, as they are today. But the focus centered somewhat obsessively on Hendrix—not only because of his playing, but also his lifestyle and lyrics. I scrounged together what I could at the time and bought a book that I have yet to see on Amazon, *Jimi Hendrix: Cherokee Mist.*

The text highlighted Jimi's writings, using pictures of his lyrics on Red Carpet Inn notepads and various envelopes. This book influenced me to write lyrics in what I now call "scribble" tablets (as discussed in Chapter 1). My original scribble tablets were those metal top-bounded 3x5s that fit in your back pocket.

Over decades, those lyrics grew into poems, short stories, character thoughts, and mindless ramblings. My 3x5 tablets evolved into Moleskines. They hold endless leads, bullet points, conversation notes, story outlines, and even book outlines—including the one you're holding now (or reading on-screen, as the case may be).

Back to 1994.

I progressed in physical health from exercise, and mental health through playing guitar and writing, all with a strict focus on a daily routine. Those routines helped me realize at a very young age that little steps produce massive results.

I've written every day since, although much was babbling (especially the endless poetry and short stories I produced in my 20s). Through this routine of writing daily, I uncovered a process that had allowed me to discover and understand what I was thinking, and who I truly was.

This routine was key in my late 20s and early 30s when words began paying the bills. For years, my most successful writing was through ghost-writing, where I made stars bigger stars, and entrepreneurs larger than life.

To date, I have ghostwritten over 500 articles for some of the world's most successful entrepreneurs and artists, including some who sold their companies for millions. Had I not established a routine early on in my writing career, none of this would have been possible (including the successful writing for ghostwriting clients).

Following a daily routine, 365 days a year, influences habits, and these habits influence your discovery as a writer and the clear communication you can offer through your words.

Again, I believe 80 percent of writing happens through experience, and the other 20 percent through the process of writing.

And neither can exist without a routine.

The routine you began now, regardless if you only wrote 1,000 words or six top-selling novels, affects every future word you will produce.

The following are some lessons I have learned over the years. And once again I put the emphasis on the modern freelance writer who makes a living from these things of discovery and communication that we call words.

Read All You Can, Whenever You Can

Read every day, from magazines to your favorite blogs to your favorite fiction writers—especially those who model clear, concise writing.

The first time I read *Fear and Loathing in Las Vegas* in my early 20s, I read straight through in one sitting. Due to my love of the simplicity of language, I've read it 10 times since.

Sometimes, I picked it up again when I needed a push into thought as I was finishing a short story or freelance articles. In most rereads, I wasn't studying the topics presented, but rather the form and structure.

I have read *Hell's Angels* (arguably Hunter S. Thompson's best work) four times, including once where I pushed a knife through the text because I was pissed at his antics near the end (more on that in Chapter 12).

Thompson's writing reads simply; it is easy to understand and enjoyable, something he certainly learned from the greats of literature like F. Scott Fitzgerald.

Michael Gerber's *The E-Myth* has the same feel, and it's also a one-sitting read. Simple and informative, it gets to the point with clean language and a flowing style that conveys its message clearly.

There are others that present much tougher challenges— Robert M. Pirsig's *Zen and the Art of Motorcycle Maintenance* and Thomas Pynchon's *Gravity's Rainbow*.

If you can get through those in one sitting and take away a simple, clear message, you're a much better reader than me.

Whatever the text, from books to blogs to food labels, read daily as part of your routine.

Find a voice you enjoy. Emulate it. But don't copy it.

Whenever you're reading, keep the phone away, and write notes in the margins of every book or magazine you're reading. If you do it digitally, highlight passages in a scribble tablet.

Your future self, and readers, will thank you.

Reread the Essential Books on Writing

Read and reread the essentials that teach writing.

Two stand out for me, one for traditional writing and one for the digital age of "short" writing: William Zinsser's *On Writing Well* and Roy Peter Clark's *How to Write Short.*

Don't just read these once. Reread them once a year. I keep editions near the proverbial throne... they're easy to grasp while nature calls.

Build (and Strengthen) Your Writing Muscles

A muscle grows when it has endless input combined with correlating relaxing points. Your writing mind works in that same way. Grow your routine of writing daily. Make writing a discipline, 365 days a year, and build those muscles.

Writing daily doesn't have to mean 4,000 words, or even 500. The routine can involve expressing morning thoughts in a scribble tablet to flesh out the sleeping thoughts, or a weird quote from a friend or something you heard in an advertisement.

Sometimes those words turn into stories, sometimes books—and other times nothing at all.

Still, this routine of writing daily will get you practicing the discipline I most love.

Think like an Olympic athlete in regards to your brain development. Don't worry about creating and sustaining a sculptured body with next-to-zero body fat; think about being able to write at a moment's notice, with great clarity and focus. Athletes are trained to perform optimally under the best and worst conditions. Writers can do this, as well.

Also, remember that waiting for inspiration or your writing muse is useless. True writers are at it every day. They develop a lifestyle that helps create inspiration and prompts that proverbial muse to surface.

In any discipline, practice is what makes it happen. It takes discipline and patience. Words simply flow better and easier once you've developed your practice and discipline. Make writing a daily part of your everyday routine, 365 days a year.

Ask Questions Daily

Friends, family, wife, children, business associates, or whomever—continually ask questions of the people around you as part of your daily routine.

You never know what you'll learn. Today, I discovered through my now five-year-old that a caterpillar's "old body" dies in a chrysalis before it is reborn with the wings of a butterfly.

The more you learn, the more you can inform and educate readers.

Questions are the highlights of learning. Let people talk and remember the 80/20 rule: let others talk 80 percent of the time *as you listen*, and *talk* only the other 20 percent.

You'll likely learn more, and your writing will likely improve.

A Routine Stable: Deadline Pressure

Hey, writers (especially you, freelancers)—let's get serious. No matter the publication, client, or publisher, deadlines matter.

Your success depends on frequent and consistent delivery, which means meeting deadlines. Every time.

I know many writers wait until the last minute for that artistic jolt that deadline pressure produces. I was one of them for over a decade.

In my night reporter days, the latest I'd be able to get a story to a copy editor was 11:30 p.m. Sometimes I'd start writing a bit after 11. Sure, the stories were only 500 words, but I worked better under pressure.

I also did this for longer pieces due to magazines and clients, though. It worked, but my stress levels were always higher leading up to that piece. If anything happened that forced me away from the work, I'd miss deadlines—and future deals with publications or clients, as a result.

Eventually, I discovered time management and productivity skills that changed all that (which we will explore in the next chapter). Don't let anyone or yourself fool you; deadlines matter.

When you meet deadlines, you appear and begin to act more professional and accomplished. Even when working on something for yourself, like a fiction novel, continue to create deadlines.

I created a deadline to finish this book within six weeks amid the COVID-19 pandemic. The deadline was based on my editor's schedule. She blocked time for the editorial process, and I needed to deliver.

Timely Communication

Besides meeting deadlines, writers must also make a routine of communicating in a timely way, especially those with clients.

By timely, I don't mean immediately, but at least within 24 hours for emails and three hours for calls or texts.

When the writing process is proactive, there's no need for reactive actions including immediate answering emails. I'm a firm believer and practitioner of only answering emails three times a day. To remain in "Deep Focus" mode (à la Cal Newport), I also keep all notifications off when working, including the phone.

Timeliness reduces stress, which equates to happiness in both work and personal situations.

Organization is Vital

Disorganization can only hold you back, especially if you're a freelancer delivering value to a client through blogging and ghostwriting.

Make organization part of your daily routine. Practice the art of self-organization, whether that means blocking certain hours daily for blog work or writing the weekly assignments across a whiteboard.

Try handwriting your tasks in a daily planner. I can't explain the psychology behind it, but physically writing stuff down helps me organize my thoughts better than any digital planner.

Do whatever works. Just make sure it's an organized system.

Embrace Criticism and Deliver Solutions

If a client or editor takes issue with the direction, voice and/or style of a piece of writing, look for solutions. Do not accept vague criticism. Make it your first reaction and part of your routine to propose solutions.

This will make your workflow smoother and less stressful. Educate clients that specific feedback drives higher quality writing and, ultimately, a better end result.

It can help to sleep on the problem before presenting the solution. Avoid getting caught in the moment and letting your emotions guide the conversation. Often, after an evening of great sleep you'll find that the problem is much more manageable than first assumed.

This is especially true for writers—I know from experience. Two decades ago, my emotions often got the best of me, especially over a criticized piece of writing.

Now, after getting away from the situation and letting my mind subconsciously do some thinking, I can see that most criticism is warranted.

Make it a routine to embrace criticism and to always provide solutions.

Document As Much As Possible

There's so much information available, but only a portion will be truly valuable and provide knowledge or expertise to your story.

When you find the valuable pieces, make a note. Copy the URL, tear the page from the magazine, write it down, or snap a pic on your smartphone.

Create a folder on your computer to keep things organized (I prefer Google Drive). I have one filled with URLs documenting everything from writing tips to amazing book reviews to motorcycle riding tips to guitar sound profiles, etc.

Make documentation a part of your daily routine and you'll save yourself much time when looking for valuable snippets of information later on.

When Freelancing, Only Work with Like-Minded Clients... Fire The Rest!

Freelancers need to think in an 80/20 style. According to Italian economist Vilfredo Pareto, we get 80 percent of the results from 20 percent of our efforts.

Richard Koch puts this principle to work in his books, particularly his masterpiece *The 80/20 Principle: The Secret to Achieving More with Less.*

You don't want that number flip-flopped, with 20 percent of results derived from 80 percent of your efforts. This can happen when you don't share the same values with your clients, whether it is a business, personal brand, or agency you're working with.

If you're writing for clients who waste your time or cause anxiety and turmoil, drop them and move on.

Thousands of clients are available to you. Make it a routine to have the patience and discipline to only work with those you believe in—and who believe in you, as well.

As an agency owner and ghostwriter for various personal brands, I've fired multiple clients.

Some are still close friends; we simply didn't agree on certain business practices such as being reactive versus proactive, or fully embracing proven content strategies.

When these disparities happen, it is kinder and ultimately better for everyone to move on.

Above All, Remember This: Writer's Block is BS!

Don't muddy your good routines with excuses about writer's block.

What to do when "writer's block" happens is one of the most common questions from new writers. I wondered about this, too—until I reframed writer's block as BS and an excuse to not write.

That's not to say there won't be times you need to delay certain aspects of the writing process.

Though I try not to, sometimes I wait until just hours before a deadline to begin a small project such as rewriting article titles and those SEO meta descriptions based on keyword research and marketing messaging.

This happens for only certain writings, and forces creativity.

When I sit down to write every day for multiple clients, I cannot afford to sit completely still and unproductive and call it writer's block.

If you are having trouble getting started and forming that first sentence, simply begin writing words. The physical and mental processes of writing can get the mind flowing.

A few tips to get words moving:

- Revisit your scribble tablets.
- Rewrite your working title in paragraph form.
- Write the ending first.
- Write down your subtopics.
- Create a stupid story around the subject you're writing.
- Brainstorm bullet points of what you would say to someone if you were talking about the topic right now.

The last point is my favorite. Imagine talking to the reader, explaining the main themes of your article, saying the words out loud.

Now type or write each bullet point. You might end up 100 bullets, or only 5 or 10. Regardless, this process helps crystallize your thoughts in the issue so you can begin writing in earnest.

You don't need to incorporate every single aspect of the aforementioned tips into your routine. However, I hope you've found at least a few ideas in this chapter to inspire you to write creatively, regularly and often.

Now, let's talk about time management and productivity thoughts for writers, two areas of focus that dramatically transformed my own writing and could have a positive impact on yours, as well.

CHAPTER 4

MODERN WRITER'S GUIDE TO TIME MANAGEMENT AND OPTIMIZATION

Back in 2008, I lost three days due to a nervous breakdown. The reasons now are clear. I had spent a decade writing fiction and music, and partying like no other while retaining full-time jobs at UPS or newspapers. I slept for a few hours a night, and didn't mind my health much.

Then, amid a breakup of a girl I dated since high school, I lost my grandfather.

Music failed. Fiction failed. Relationships failed. Life failed for a loved one.

And so did my mental stability.

This led directly to a breakdown, and a refocus on life.

Shortly after I took that nervous breakdown, I got serious about writing and business - a business, of course, created around writing.

I also became obsessed with optimizing time and enhancing productivity.

Most of us have long-term goals; the problem is that we tend to lack the day-to-day focus to make those goals a reality.

It's easy to set a goal that's five years away. "I have lots of time." Days go by and turn into months, then years, and suddenly not much (if anything) has been done to move you any closer to that goal.

It's easy to sideline daily tasks when you have *all of this time* in the future to make progress.

I was a culprit, which forced me to figure out time management methods that actually work. I called the process that came out of much trial and error and experimentation "365 to Vision: Time Management Inverted" (and am wrapping up a book of the same title).

It is modeled upon the inverted pyramid used in journalism where the top, widest tier is the most important, and everything below supports what's above.

These four tiers of systemized time management for ultimate productivity are:

- One year to reach your long-term vision or goal
- 12 monthly alignments
- 52 weeks of tactics
- 365 days of tasks

Of course, those numbers can change with the size of your vision. If your goal is to write a book within six months, cut those numbers in half. If the vision is a five-year goal, the top three tiers can grow.

For most writers, it is the day-to-day tasks carried out 365 days a year that help us truly achieve our goals in the smoothest and less stressful way. My "Time Management Inverted" manuscript is plotted out over two years, for example.

As for this book, I had initially planned to write it over three months. Due to COVID-19, it turned into six weeks of consecutive Wednesday nights spent drafting and a final day of edits.

Whatever your timeline, organizing it so that you make progress daily enables you to keep your eye on both the big picture and the immediate tasks at hand.

It helps to simplify, reduce stress, and make the writing process easier when you have these quick wins each day that feed your goal. Each month, check your progress against your expectations. Realign if necessary to achieve your long-term goal.

This 365 to Vision concept has helped me develop day-to-day routines that, when practiced diligently, turn into the good habits that increase productivity.

The underlying theme is simple—create positive, proactive habits. In reality, we know that it takes time and effort to make new habits stick.

The common consensus is that you can form a new habit in 21 days, a figure from Maxwell Maltz's *PsychoCybernetics*. But that book was published in 1960; more recent studies by

University College London[4] say some can form a new habit in as little as two months, though others take over eight months.

Whether a habit can be formed in 21 days or eight months is beside the point. There is no magic number of times you will complete a task and suddenly find it effortless.

You will work at writing 365 days a year and in doing so, will make it a habit. But first, you need to make room for it. In the 365 to Vision thought process for writers, productive habit formation begins with optimizing your day-to-day time management by ceasing the daily activities that hold you back.

These distracting, dysfunctional habits keep you in a reactive vs proactive state, hampering productivity and dampening creativity. Rid your routine of the following habits to increase your likelihood of time management success.

Neurotically Checking Email

This is the top productivity-killer for many writers.

I've seen this in both office and remote work situations, and was once a culprit myself. When you neurotically and frequently check emails, you keep yourself in a reactive mode of thinking about and responding to things that *usually* don't matter at that moment.

---

[4] https://onlinelibrary.wiley.com/doi/full/10.1002/ejsp.674

Begin with turning off email notifications to reduce the sights and sounds that distract you from your writing.

Schedule periods of time (the shorter the better) each day to check and respond to emails, and make it a habit only to check at those times. How many of these email periods you need to schedule per day depends on the day's workflow and your volume of email.

On my editing days, for example, and on nights dedicated to spew and first drafts, email is completely sidelined. I check email only once I've completed at least three hours of writing or editing. I may even turn on my "away" autoresponder and notify people to call my personal cell if things need to be addressed immediately.

Another tip I learned from the late Chet Holmes, author of *The Ultimate Sales Machine* (a book everyone should read regardless of career choice), is to only open the emails you can commit to at that moment (more on him in Chapter 11).

Holmes writes: "If you touch it, take action. That's the first step to great time management. Don't open that email until you're ready to deal with it."

If you really cannot deal with it right away, add the action item to your prioritized list (more on that later).

Try it; it's a game-changer.

No Call to Action in Subject Lines

One more quick thought on emails to reserve focus when writing.

If you're sending an email, make sure the subject line says exactly what you expect in response: "Edits Needed on Article by April 20."

Also, at the end of the email add a "p.s." that asks them to change the subject line when replying. Following the example above, ask them to reply: "RE: Edits Completed on November SEJ Article."

Make this a habit, and influence others to do the same. Also demand that those emails only address what the subject line intends; if the email's content changes, either note it in the rewritten subject line or start an entirely new thread.

This small habit will not only save time, but also much frustration when searching for a subject within emails.

Neurotically Checking Social Media

I'm a victim of this, especially when there are newsworthy events happening. Soon, I'm sucked into reading every response on a post, which naturally leads to the formation of opinions and responses. Thirty minutes may pass and I'm then behind schedule on whatever it is I was working on.

These are just bad habits, but they are tough ones to break.

Like emails, shut off all social notifications on any electronic device. Reward yourself every few hours with a quick check on social updates, but allocate as little time as possible and make it less each time.

Remember to install an app that tracks your on-phone time activity, and to make it a routine to check those stats daily. You'd be surprised at how much time you waste looking at your Facebook app every once in a while throughout the day.

Take your weekly social activity, and multiply it by 52. That's a lot of hours to be gawking at what people are saying about you, or caring about what others are doing.

Becoming Attached to Phone and Texts

Having your phone nearby while writing is a psychological tease and next to email and social media, text messaging is the third-largest distraction. It's too easy to pick up the phone and begin texting when you feel frustrated or unmotivated.

There is one simple way to defeat all of this: keep notifications off (yes, that's an ongoing theme!) and hide your phone in a drawer or face-down. In more creative times when I don't want to be bothered by anything, I'll make sure all notifications are off. Sometimes I simply put my phone into airplane mode or keep it out of the office.

I typically use my Mac's iMessage and FaceTime apps during work hours for phone calls and texts, which makes my phone useless. During long intervals of focused writing, I keep the notifications on these programs off, as well. I turn them back on when checking my emails or taking a break.

Embracing Other Distractions

I work from a home office, and someone is building a house a few lots up from me. It's super annoying but for the past few days, I've simply turned up the music. Music (especially music I'm not familiar with) helps me focus while writing.

For others, this may not be the case; do what is necessary to eliminate or at least reduce external distractions. Try working from another area of the office, moving to a local cafe, or— I used to do when under deadline amidst an office loaded with distractions—work in the car (with music, of course).

For writers in agency or in-house situations—let coworkers know they can't bother you at any time or just pop in to ask a question. You're not being mean or antisocial; you're simply setting boundaries that allow you to get quality work completed in a more timely manner. (If you are going to block off writing time in this way, be sure to make it clear that you are open for colleagues to ask questions any other time. Use a colored paper on your desk or some other simple indicator that enables colleagues to easily see when you prefer not to be distracted.)

Not Creating a Prioritized Day-to-Day Tasks List

Back to Chet Holmes and *The Ultimate Sales Machine*.

Holmes says that without a day-to-day list of actionable items, you'll likely always be in reactive mode. He advocates that you should have, at most, six items you must complete each day.

I agree, though I would add that you can shrink that to as little as two or three tasks per day when working through larger pieces of writing that consume more time and concentration.

If you are a freelancer and working on multiple projects, make it a habit to prioritize daily writing tasks from the most to least important. I used to put off the most important writing tasks until the end of the day, but found that either the work felt sloppy or I simply didn't possess the creative energy I had in the mornings.

This is psychological; I was trying not to get to that most important thing because I simply didn't want to do it. Everything before it took longer.

When you prioritize your most to least important writing, you take those small wins and stay fresh for the bigger tasks. Your ideas are much clearer and you avoid that fatigue of having the biggest task of the day looming over you.

Not Blocking Time

Now that you have a prioritized list, block time for each writing task. Times allotted will be different for everyone, but try never to block more than two hours for any single task without taking at least a 10-15-minute break.

Again, each writer's comfort level here is different. I can go five hours, at most, when completing a writing assignment that needs super focus (or "hyperfocus," as I explain later).

I typically break this time up with a 10- to 15-minute break for an espresso, checking on the news and social feeds, and bouncing around on the little trampoline I have in my office.

When I return to the stand-up writing desk and get back to it, it takes about 15 minutes to regain my fully-focused rhythm. Don't forget to allocate this time into your blocks.

A quick example of a typical day's list of blocked time for my days that are dedicated to editing and drafting might look something like this:

- 6:30-7 a.m.: Check/respond to emails
- 7-9:30 a.m.: Edit Forbes draft
- 9:30-9:45 a.m.: Espresso, catch up on news
- 9:45-11:45 a.m.: Continue editing Forbes Draft
- 11:45-noon: Revisit scribble tablets of outlines created for Forbes Draft
- Noon-12:30 p.m.: Read current book
- 12:30-1 p.m.: Check/respond to emails
- 1-2 p.m.: Workout/lunch
- 2-3:30 p.m.: Create outlines or work first drafts of an article

- 3:30-4 p.m.: Check/respond to emails
- 4-5 p.m.: Final edits on Forbes draft
- 5-5:30 p.m.: Prioritize tomorrow's workflow; revisit monthly calendar

Note: I also hand-write these down in my weekly planner. I spend so much time behind the screen that the little act of physically writing simplifies things for me.

Not Creating Monthly/Weekly High-Level Lists

Shortly after launching my content marketing agency, I scheduled the first half-hour of every day to create my daily tasks list.

As more responsibilities piled on, including writing for books and articles, I needed more organization to focus on the longer-term goals for each month over the day-to-day tasks. This led to a new habit of creating monthly and weekly lists of higher-level items to tackle.

On the first weekday of every month, I'll block two hours to prioritize what high-level weekly tactics I need to achieve for that month, such as articles due or meetings.

This is where it's smart to check your monthly meeting/call calendar and make sure to pencil them in immediately (again, I truly "pencil" things in).

Planning a Meeting without an Agenda

This is again focused on the freelancers and businesspeople with client meetings.

Freelancers and businesspeople know that a meeting without an agenda is useless. Weekly meetings with no agenda run the risk of becoming fluff sessions for those doing well, and bitching sessions for those doing poorly. I've seen this often, and it's not pretty.

Everyone typically walked out frustrated and needed another half hour to relax before getting back to real work.

I've had clients who wanted hour-long monthly calls just to check on things. Some did it out of pure curiosity and to understand progress (a good thing), but for others it was just a way to track what they were paying for (not such a good use of time).

I was proactive and began making agendas for these calls. Today, some of these calls barely last 15 minutes, and both sides leave the conversation happy. Transparent project management aids in saving time on calls, because the client knows exactly what's happening and when.

Plan your meetings with a clear agenda and include an outline in your meeting invite. Always have one person lead. That doesn't mean it's their meeting; rather, they are tracking and monitoring time, which brings us to the next point.

Not Embracing a 2-Minute Rule During Meetings

As every meeting should have an agenda and an appointed person monitoring, each meeting should also go by the two-minute rule. Whoever has the floor to talk or constructively debate gets exactly two minutes to make their point before another person takes over.

This eliminates back-to-back banter between opposing opinions (typically based on emotion, not logic) and allows people time to think before expressing an opinion. It helps keep discussion focused on one topic so progress can be made and the group can move on together.

Once you make a habit of setting agendas, meetings get much shorter. If you have a client meeting planned for two hours, create a strict agenda and shorten it. If it's a half-hour call with a client to discuss strategy, again, create a strict agenda and shorten that meeting.

Long meetings are a waste of time. If you have a meeting planned for an hour with a strict agenda and finish in 40 minutes, that leaves 20 minutes of spare time to get an early jump on another project or put towards daydreaming (something we'll discuss soon).

Make it known that you don't want to waste time. If people want to waste working hours talking, they can always meet for a drink after work.

Ridding your routine of the above habits takes a big chunk out of most people's productivity issues by cutting out the distractions and time wasters that hold us back. Now, see if you can get more granular.

Avoid Getting Hung Up on Either the Big or Small Pictures

Unity of focus on both the big and small pictures is a must, hence the practice of having day-to-day tasks that:

- make up weekly tactics that...
- feed into monthly goals that...
- need to be realigned over and over to...
- achieve your long-term goal(s).

Make it a habit to see and consider both the big and small pictures as you complete tasks and realign. This habit will help you retain focus and worth through your short- and long-term goals with less stress.

Get "Hyperfocused"

One of my favorite reads on productivity is Chris Bailey's *Hyperfocus: How to be More Productive in a World of Distractions*. How can you, as a writer, deliberately manage your attention?

Bailey says our minds wander, on average, 47 percent of the day. This is due to our brain's vulnerability toward distraction. In recognizing and being mindful of what is managing our attention and what tasks we can control, we can become more productive writers and do more in less time.

Bailey says there are four types of tasks:

- **Necessary Work:** Unattractive yet Productive (team meetings and quarterly budgets)
- **Unnecessary Work:** Unattractive and Unproductive (rearranging your desk, procrastinating)
- **Distracting Work:** Attractive yet Unproductive (checking social media, reading news, etc.)
- **Purposeful Work:** Attractive and Productive (tasks with the largest impact, most engaging tasks)

The goal here is to become more deliberate about managing your attention and focusing on the *Purposeful* and *Necessary* writing, and slowing focus on distracting and unnecessary work.

Of course, this is just an extremely high-level look at the principles in *Hyperfocus*. Read the book; it'll help your focus and ease stress in both work writing and personal writing.

Take Multiple Daily Breaks

When we discussed creating daily lists above, short breaks were always included.

I typically find myself distracted after two solid hours of focus. A short 10- or 15-minute break diverts the mind's attention and allows for a refresh.

This need for short breaks is especially important when in a creative stage of writing. A few things that work to divert my attention are music, motorcycle rides, reading fiction, or taking a short hike/walk.

Find what works for you, but remember to take breaks throughout the day (especially those who work from home that continually grind).

As you master more and more of these time management lessons, fewer breaks will be needed throughout the day. You will find that you can hold your focus for greater periods.

Take Extended Periods of Time for Unplugging

This is as important as your daily breaks from writing. Each week, take time to totally get away from it all.

I do this religiously every Wednesday evening unless I'm traveling on business. This may be a "spirited" motorcycle ride that demands hyperfocus (because without hyperfocus, at triple-digit speeds I could die).

It doesn't allow headspace for being bored or dwelling on work issues or overthinking the writing I had been working on. You might try a long hike, play guitar, wrench on motorcycles, or plant a garden—anything that physically takes you away from the process of writing.

I also hide the phone during these times and don't check emails, social feeds, texts, etc.

Another habit I've been working on is totally unplugging from electronics for certain periods such as dinner hour or the two hours before sleep every night. On Sundays, my ultimate goal is to completely avoid opening a computer or using a phone. I've only achieved this 15 times in the past three years but when I did, Mondays were super refreshed and productive.

Getting away from it all keeps the mind fresh, especially for the working writers who must pay bills with their craft. Find your threshold of creativity daily and give yourself permission to walk away from it all when the writing isn't flowing easily or feels sloppy.

Ask Questions

We just briefly touched on this in the previous chapter on routines, but there's another important reason to ask a lot of questions.

Spending too much time poking around an unfamiliar subject or concept can be a real productivity killer. Oftentimes, spending just a short time asking questions of a subject matter expert can help you get up to speed much quicker. You learn the best direction in which to take your research and can save time you would have spent just trying to learn the basics.

Many people are afraid to ask questions because they think they might seem dumb. They may hear enough to be intrigued, but wait until after the conversation to immediately go read up on the subject.

As the founder of Bridgewater, Ray Dalio, says in his book *Principles*, everyone has the "right and responsibility to try to make sense of important things."

Dalio says if you feel awkward, you should bluntly say, "Let's agree that I am a dumb shit but I still need to make sense of this, so let's move slowly to make sure that happens."

One of the quickest ways to learn is to ask questions and listen with an open mind. The more knowledge you have, the easier future writing will become, and the more time you will save. And believe me, no one expects you to know everything.

Attempt to Master Writing

When I teach writing, I tell everyone to continually *attempt to master writing* even though I believe that mastery of any type, especially writing, is virtually impossible.

In fact, if you think you are getting close, it means you are becoming complacent and need to push yourself more.

Complacency is the ultimate killer for any type of creative work - especially writing. Once you become extremely fluid with your words, it's time to change.

Discover a different angle. Pick a minor topic within your writing and expand on it. Learn a different perspective about the subject.

If you're going to *attempt* to master writing, never stop pushing yourself to discover something new. Just make sure that new thought is equally fascinating to both you *and* the reader.

Stop Waiting for Inspiration

This is just another form of procrastination. Get writing during your most creative periods. Yours will be very different from mine, as each writer's most creative times occur at drastically different times.

This can be attributed to our circadian rhythms, lifestyle choices and more, but we won't get too scientific here.

Some people don't kick into full creative mode in those typical work hours of 9 to 5, which is why I've personally never adhered to those hours. For some, their most serious work happens after 10 a.m. or around noon. Some of the best writers I know swear by writing in the afternoons and evenings.

Find what works for you, and do your most creative writing within that period at the same time, every day.

Note that these creative periods may change over time, as they did for me. I was once midnight to 5 a.m. writer. These days, I complete more quality work in the early mornings (usually well before my five-year-old son, Enzo, awakens and again shortly after he goes off to Pre-K). Hanging out with him in the mornings is my timed break and helps refresh my mind between writing tasks.

I slip into late-night/early morning creative writing at certain times and still embrace that. But those days mess with the flow of the weeks, so I only participate in those early-morning periods sporadically.

Live a Healthy Lifestyle

You simply can't get away from the reality that if you don't feel your best, you're not going to produce your best writing.

See those people nodding off in the middle of the day? Something is not serving them well, whether it's a lack of sleep or an unhealthy diet.

Whether it's your diet, exercise, sleeping pattern, or some other area that needs work, the solution is often something we already know.

But it can be difficult to achieve due to our psychological barriers to change. This is why it's so important, once again, to make the better behavior into a habit.

Every solution is different for everyone, and some will be a hybrid mix of what works. For example, just ahead of starting my business—when I needed every ounce of mental and physical energy for both work and my toddler—I discovered Dave Asprey's "Bulletproof Diet" and Tim Ferris' "4-Hour Workweek."

I took aspects from both, among other books, and created my own personalized plan that simply worked.

Create a lifestyle of healthy habits, and your writing productivity will increase dramatically.

Continue Your Daily Writing Education (Yes, Again!)

Read books on writing. Take seminars. Take online classes.

Do whatever it takes and *NEVER* stop learning and improving your craft of writing.

Again, complacency is the ultimate killer of creativity. It also will crush your mind from growing, and slow your words down.

Protest any form of becoming stale in new learning. The more you know, the quicker and more proficiently you will write.

I ended this chapter with health and education for a reason. Without good health, your brain cannot operate at full capacity. And without maintaining that constant state of learning, you become complacent and progress halts.

Without good health and knowledge, it's nearly impossible to become the best person—and writer—you can possibly be.

Now let's turn from lifestyle to journalism, a discipline that can help keep your storytelling sharp, 365 days a year—all the way through to reaching your vision.

Chapter 5

Modern Writer's Guide to Journalism

Storytime.

My path through college wasn't traditional and neither was my career path, which I'll discuss quickly.

Sometimes in writing, you just let the words go and tell the story for you. In life, sometimes we do the same with the everyday twists and turns we encounter.

At 18, I took a job at the UPS docks loading trucks during the evenings.

This was after six years in catering, during which I sometimes found myself delivering food to million-dollar homes. I was the driver at 14. The other workers sat on crates in the caterer's gray minivan, stinking of exhaust fumes intermingled with spilled rigatoni, meatballs, or chicken gravy.

I turned 21 in the year 2000 and shortly after my September birthday, a year before 9/11, I began driving for Big Brown. I studied journalism at a local community college, where I met two teachers with the talent to actually, *truly* teach writing.

I argue to this day that they would do better at major universities, but I am thankful they were there for me in my early years as a writer.

Prompted by a three-week cross-country trip with my dear friend (and influenced by Kerouac and more serious music by then), I left UPS when I was 23. My Associates in Journalism landed me a job at a local newspaper, where I went from making serious money for a youngster (drivers back then made $20 an hour) to absolute shit. My salary was cut in half, but I wanted to write.

My family and many friends were in an uproar. Why would I walk away from a job I can work for 30 years and retire comfortably with full benefits?

I began in obituary writing, of all things, which taught me valuable lessons on reporting correct information. Nothing is worse than pissing off a family in their most vulnerable time. My position grew to the night reporter, and I began freelancing on the side to earn extra cash.

(I was also studying literature in a private university, playing guitar in a local band, and drinking and partying like a proverbial rockstar. That lifestyle is reflected in the fiction I also wrote during those years. But that's another LONG story.)

Freelancing led me to a content marketing manager position at a pet supply company, a Fortune 500 company back then. I only lasted nine months at that place, an experience I wrote about in a poem titled, "9 Months of Corporate Pregnancy."

That was around the same time I broke up with my girlfriend of 12 years and had a nervous breakdown. Waking up to realize you've lost three days of your life calls for drastic changes.

I told corporate America to go screw itself and decided that writing was the answer to everything I needed out of life, both work and personal. During that time, though, amid a breakup and breakdown, I also met the girl who would become my wife and mother to my child.

It goes without saying that I got more value than ever out of those experiences.

Cue another nearly eight-year stint at UPS. I figured I'd write fiction and drive a big brown truck, Charles Bukowski style.

But I also worked my ass off to get into the motorcycle industry, motorcycles being the only other things besides words and music that got me through the day.

I sent stories and pitches to every magazine in the motorcycle industry for four months before I got up the nerve to cold-call *Cycle World* in 2008.

Finally, I was in! They accepted a piece on safety lessons learned at UPS, which I translated to motorcyclists. It was a short, 300-word safety article. That became the basis for a motorcycle safety book I'm currently working on, but more importantly, it lent me the clout to talk to other publications.

I had offers to move to California and work with the most known moto publications but found one that was thinking digitally at the time: *Ultimate Motorcycling*. In three months, I was hired as Online Editor (a position I hold to this day).

I knew nothing about SEO back then but got a quick education after getting hacked by a digital marketing agency around 2010 as the website moved from Drupal to WordPress.

I found another calling—digital marketing—and decided to learn all I could about SEO, which led to further movement and the next middle finger to UPS.

I joined an agency and stayed just long enough to learn what *not* to do as a company owner and businessman. I fled in late 2016, launched ContentMender[5] officially in March 2017, and haven't looked back since.

Although it's been a while since I've written an obituary, all of this stemmed from that early career in journalism.

Writing is my core focus, and will always be my core focus. In many years of writing, I've built great relationships with many writers, the best of whom also came from journalism backgrounds.

I will never forget that my true start in words that paid (not the poetry I wrote around lyrics in my early 20s) began in journalism, something which has undoubtedly shaped the way I run my

---

[5] https://contentmender.com/

agency today. I spent five years as a night reporter making $24K (and that was after two years of raises).

Though the pay was beyond horrible, I needed to learn how to write in real-time and complete these tasks quickly due to nightly deadlines. I had no clue that a host of other skills I was developing at the time would serve me so well over the course of my writing career.

I love the journalism field so much I never left it - even after launching my agency. As I said above, I remain at *Ultimate Motorcycling*, traveling the world to ride and review motorcycles.

Last year, I read another one of those books "I should have read years ago" —Joe Pulizzi's *Epic Content Marketing*. He says that the most successful businesses (think Coca-Cola, Proctor & Gamble, Adobe) think like traditional media companies rather than mere sellers of products or services.

I couldn't agree more. After working in media for two decades, I see how loyal readers can be if engaging and valuable content marketing efforts are present.

And the best way forward? Taking advantage of the unique skill set that journalists can offer.

I'll break down some of the most important here.

Learn The "Five W's and How"

From day one, every journalist learns to rely on the "Five W's and How":

- Who
- What
- When
- Where
- Why
- How

I like to think of this as 5W1H, a super simple formula that allows journalists to gather all necessary information during research. All six elements must be answered for any type of writing to truly express what I call TAR —Trust, Authority, and Reputation—as a writer.

This formula is a must when gathering data or interviewing a source. While most interviews are on the phone, through a chat, or via online conference software like Google Chat or Skype, in-person, face-to-face interviews will always produce the best results.

When 5W1H is covered, your research has all of the material needed to answer questions and solve problems relevant to the reader, which are the two main factors all written content requires.

For modern content to be successful, each piece—whether a blog, service page, guest blog, memorandum, or novel—should answer all six questions.

In journalism, the *who, what, why,* and *how* are foundational. If these are not covered, the message has little chance of resonating with your readers.

With that said, for the digital marketing landscape, you'll find that some types of writing—think product copy or blogs—need more of a "2Ws and One H" approach.

The who, when, and where of traditional journalism are typically answered on the company bio page or footer, making them redundant if included in other copy. But the *why, what* and *how* are always a must. Explain *why* to capture an emotion, then use *what* and *how* to rationalize it.

Always Start with Why

In *Start with Why* (more than one million copies sold), TED superstar and one of my all-time favorite thinkers, Simon Sinek says, "People don't buy WHAT you do, they buy WHY you do it. A failure to communicate WHY creates nothing but stress or doubt."

In business, much writing tends to focus solely on the *how* and *what* of the product or service. We focus on the features, prices, and everything that makes one thing different from another.

Many experts will tell you this is the information you need for a successful web presence.

But this approach fails to recognize the emotional aspect of reading by first asking *why*. The *how* and *what* are absolutely needed, but as a rational follow-up to the more emotionally *why*.

The *why* in any piece of business writing should be immediately apparent.

Apple does this really well.

Apple doesn't just sell MacBook Pros; the brand and its products inspire human creativity.

You can read this loud and clear in the latest MacBook Pro page copy. It immediately answers the *why* of the product by highlighting "A Touch of Genius," and is followed by the typical *how* and *what*.

Another genius Apple campaign that begins with the *why* is that old, simple iPhone 4 ad: "This Changes Everything. Again."

Writing that asks *why* first naturally appeals to a prospect's emotions, and influences the three elements of TAR (trust, authority, and reputation) that can begin a lifelong relationship with a reader or customer.

"Can begin" are the crucial words here because the *why* must be backed up with a solid What and How. Here's, um, why.

Once you appeal to the emotional side of the reader, it's time to back up those feelings with rational data. That's where the what and how are utilized.

Remember: The *what* and the *how* are vital, but should always follow the *why*. Appeal to emotion first; follow with rationale.

Inverted Pyramid Style

This is another tool from the world of journalism that is especially effective when writing blogs (which are typically skimmed through by people with zero attention span).

When you write content like a blog, layer the information in an inverted pyramid with the most important information first and all supporting details below. Not all blogs need this, but it works for most.

Start with a catchy introduction and immediately tell the reader what the article is about. Why should they keep reading?

Include the right keywords and you'll be able to snatch up featured snippets (those questions or blocks of highlighted content at the top of the search results page) much easier.

Who You Ask is As Important as What You Ask

This one is for freelancers and agency writers who are creating content for clients.

Who you ask is just as important as the questions you are asking. Most of the agencies I worked with dealt only with the marketing departments of bigger businesses, though in some smaller businesses other teams were involved.

To obtain the most vital and unique information, writers should speak with not only the marketing team but the CEOs, founders, sales teams, and any of those on the proverbial frontline who deal with day-to-day customer relations.

Each can provide unique insight and perspective that adds rich detail for readers. And the more varied perspective you have, the easier it is for readers to understand the *why*.

Credibility & Factual Correctness

Journalists earn respect through their credibility and use of factual content. (And you can lose credibility just as quickly being caught out publishing misinformation or untruths.)

The best journalists take the extra time to triple-check facts, especially those from online sources. They interview and cite only the most reputable experts on the topic at hand.

Writing based on loose facts immediately dilutes the authority not only of that piece of content but also the brand hosting it. Imagine what a freelance writer can do to a business reputation with sloppy reporting.

For your writing to be successful, credibility is key.

Clarity

What touched on clarity in Chapter 1 and revisit it now from the journalist's perspective.

The best journalists aren't just relaying information; they take the dull and make it energetic. This has much to do with the particular journalist's style of writing, but also requires a good dose of clarity, which is necessary in order to deliver their information to the widest audience possible.

Clarity means answering the 5 Ws and How without resorting to using jargon, idioms, or other potentially confusing embellishments.

Of course, if you're working for a medical journal and are speaking to a dermatologist, you can use words like hydradermabrasion or microdermabrasion.

But the typical audience for most businesses—prospects that are out to learn—need the information presented in a clear and simple manner.

Balance

How many websites do you visit with content written from a "me, me, me," perspective? So many are focused on their own accolades, rewards, services, and products.

This type of writing immediately throws a site visitor off balance. They came looking for a solution to their unique problem but are left wondering, *What about me*?

Great writing immediately puts energy into the reader by addressing their needs, questions, or problems.

With that said, businesses still have to give their products or services exposure. But even on product pages, there needs to be a balance of product/service information and value to the reader.

Journalists understand balance; there are always multiple sides to every story, and to convey a credible message there must be a representation of all sides.

Understand Your Audience

Content is useless without a targeted audience and nobody knows this better than a journalist—especially a niche-based journalist.

Reputable journalists are trained to understand their audience and write for them. That means creating a voice that appeals to that target audience, and always knowing what questions and problems that the audience is having.

Good journalists use tools to find their target audience and all the questions that are being asked. Spend a moment on Reddit or Quora and you'll have hundreds of questions and topics to get your mind working.

Storytelling: It's Needed!

Storytelling through content is nothing new. The first figurative cave paintings were from the Upper Paleolithic period—about 40,000 years ago—and told simple stories about everyday life in that era.

Society thrives on storytelling. Think about the most popular Netflix series, or the storylines behind famous athletes like Michael Jordan or Ted Bundy.

The same goes for businesses. If you can create a storyline to go along with the valuable information you want to convey to readers across various mediums, you can engage and entertain instead of just relaying the facts.

Journalists practice storytelling every day, and so should you. Bring a voice and face to your client's businesses through good old, proven storytelling.

Deadlines Matter

Journalists must deal with deadlines, sometimes on a daily basis. Writing to meet deadlines is another learned skill that forces you to focus and think clearly to get the best work completed in the least amount of time.

Once learned and mastered, this skill provides endless value to your writing plans. If you create project deadlines and need things like copy or video, you'll make sure they are complete and polished before the deadline.

And they must be *real* deadlines. I used to make "soft" deadlines for myself, thinking it would allow me to finish a project earlier and in better quality, but the real deadline always looms—even if it's subconsciously.

For those who edit or manage freelance writers, here's an expert tip. You need to create earlier deadlines for those working with you, as well. Leave yourself time to complete edits or rework with the writer before the content is due to the client.

Learn to Deal with a Process Controlled by Editors

"Editors are licensed to be curious."

- William Zinsser

A seamless editorial process is a must for businesses serious about content. This goes for any type of content production, from blogs to video content to infographics.

For example, my blog business's writing projects go through seven layers with separate editors for each:

- SEO provides keyword research
- Content Strategist provides the writers with overall main points and optimized subtopics based on working with SEO
- SEO provides SEO guidelines to writers with related keywords/subtopics
- Writing process
- Editing Process
- SEO Enhancement Process
- Final on-Page SEO/Editorial Process

Throughout any of those seven layers, some criticism will go back and forth, but it's all to deliver only top-quality work to the client. Like a journalist, learn to take criticism.

The more eyes, the better on any writing project. Sometimes those furthest removed from one process can quickly find a mistake or recognize an improvement in another.

One more thought for business owners.

When a business begins fulfilling its content needs, a journalist is the farthest thing from mind. Most put ads out for copywriters, designers, or blog writers to fulfill their needs.

These businesses are missing out on the many advantages and value that the modern journalist can deliver.

From knowing what information is needed to balancing content to creating strict editorial calendars, journalists can help a business scale quickly, and achieve success with credibility.

And above all tell one great story along the way.

Frequent and Consistent Content/Editorial Calendars

One of the biggest productivity secrets is creating blocks of time for a specific task. Some people have endless to-do lists, and others block out time for client work.

I worked with an SEO once who always announced and shared his number of to-dos at the end of the day. His list was up to 150 to-dos at one point! I'm sure 80% of those were useless tasks that could have been diced or delegated, but that's for another book.

Either way, that's absurd. If you don't give your to-do item in a block of time and have the discipline to follow this out daily, that to-do list will only grow—and likely with some added stress and weight.

Top journalists think in a similar way when creating their content calendars. Frequency and consistency are keys to strong writing, which keeps the storyline moving along smoothly.

Do the same with your content creation calendar. I work with companies that create yearly or quarterly calendars, and others that go month-to-month due to the nature of their changing business.

Regardless of how far ahead you want to plan, have a content calendar for each blog, guest blog, social media posts, or video, etc., you'll produce. The best content marketing campaigns are built upon strict frequency and consistency. Do the same if you want to have long-term success.

Super Focus

Journalists sometimes must complete writing tasks within a limited amount of time to keep the story, well... timely.

Learn to kill distractions and get super focused. I wrote about increasing productivity in chapters 3 and 4, and all of those habits I discuss allow one to become super focused and get more quality work completed in less time (and with less stress).

Check out Cal Newport's book *Deep Work*. He gets seriously deep into becoming super focused.

With a few thoughts on how journalism practices can improve your writing life, it's time to provide a small chapter on the essentials of SEO for writers. Knowing even the basics of SEO can change the game for modern writers.

CHAPTER 6

THE SEO ESSENTIALS

Search Engine Optimization (SEO) was not even in my vocabulary until 2007. That was the year I began submitting to various digital publications with a goal of living the freelancer lifestyle.

As part of my studies on submitting the best copy possible, I began learning about SEO and how it affects website traffic.

My thought process was simple: the better the SEO, the more traffic my content will attract, the more people will read my articles, and ultimately, the more work I'll have.

That SEO education, along with my writing experience, led to an opportunity as head of content for the marketing department of a local pet company that was then a Fortune 200 company.

While there, I continued freelancing and studying writing and SEO, which led to my position as Online Editor at *Ultimate Motorcycling*, multiple lucrative freelance writing work, and eventually, the launch of my SEO-driven content marketing company.

I found back then that other freelance writers I knew were not interested in SEO, which provided an opportunity for my work to rise above the noise. Even today, many writers are uninterested in or misunderstand SEO.

If you're one of those non-believers of SEO or hate tech (like me), stay with me here!

SEO is crucial for those writing for any type of digital publication. Understanding even the basics gives you a serious edge over your freelance competition. (For the tech Luddites, don't worry—we're not going to get technical.)

I know you came here for writing and SEO has nothing to do with writing books, poetry, or short stories for magazines. But if you have just expressed your most amazing storytelling and want to teach a valuable lesson to the world, you must realize that most read digitally.

What's a story worth if it can't be found online and only through word of mouth?

When consulting with my established writing friends—even some involved within the SEO industry—many asked me to place this chapter next to last.

These consultations tried proving their whys. For my friends involved in SEO, this material appears basic. For those not involved in SEO, this material appears boring.

But SEO matters - more so for the writers who don't care. If a searcher on Google can't find your story, how many lives can you truly affect?

Again, it's all about value and process. If you want to reach the widest audiences possible (even if you're a *Forbes* or *NYT* staff member), SEO matters.

Whether you're blogging for the local motorcycle parts store or writing product copy for Walmart or telling the way it truly is on your personal blog, SEO matters.

If you do any digital writing and you submit or publish content optimized for search, you're 1,000 steps ahead.

Mix that optimized content with all traditional elements of writing, and you'll earn more respect (and money) than the others.

Think Keywords First

Your writing must be discovered before you can have any impact.

No matter how intelligent they have become, search engine algorithms can't yet recognize the best voice in a piece of writing.

If keywords (and other clues such as people linking to your work) are there, you have the opportunity to be found in search.

Digital marketers know the importance of keyword research. Yet for some reason, much content is published without proper keyword research and a clear keyword strategy (which includes optimizing each page or post for target keywords).

Publications like *Search Engine Journal, Moz,* and *Search Engine Land* offer hundreds of articles on keyword research. They are a great place to start to build your knowledge on this foundation for SEO success.

With proper research, you'll know your target keyword volume and trends and can optimize your post or page to capitalize on those opportunities.

For example, unless a website you're writing for has a powerful online authority (such as the leaders of any industry), ranking for high-volume, "short-tail" keywords— those with 1,000 or more monthly searches per month, for example—is going to be incredibly tough. It would be much easier to rank for a lower-volume, "long-tail" keyword with 100 searches per month.

A quick example of short-tail and long-tail keywords: "Ducati Motorcycles" is short-tail; 2020 Ducati Panigale V4 Specs" is long-tail.

Your main service pages, or "parent pages," can chase the higher volume keywords. Allow the other lower "child" pages, especially blogs and educational articles, to chase long-tail, lower-volume keywords that are typically endless in any industry.

Don't Forget 'Related' Keywords

During your keyword research, you'll also discover related keywords that, when properly implemented, will show relevancy to the post/page's target keyword(s) and theme.

For example, if your target keyword for an article is "blog writing tips," some related keywords (according to my go-to tool, SEMrush) are "blog content writing tips," "blog post tips," and "how to write better blogs."

Spend time creating this list of related keywords. It is vital to your overall strategy.

Don't simply stuff keywords into your content after doing the writing.

If you're well prepared with keyword research, have the list of semantically connected keywords in view as you write.

Insert related keywords naturally. The more expertise you have on a subject, the easier this natural insertion becomes.

I'd bet many of these related keywords are already in place for experts in most of their work, but a quick search for others will help the search value of that article. And being reminded of these related keywords helps spawn new ideas for writers.

Approach Keyword Research Like an Art

There are thousands of keyword research articles available. Research, discover, and test what works best for you.

Make this process cyclical. I build content calendars out in three-month segments, performing fresh keyword research at the beginning of every cycle. Industries change and new keywords trend quicker than you might expect.

Study the Competition for Keywords

There are a lot of different tools you can use to find competitor keywords, which can give you major insight into what keywords are working for others.

Warning: *only* steal keywords. Don't study the actual writing of your competitors. Once you do that, you sound like them and struggle to create anything original.

You can target the same keywords but you do not want to sound like you have regurgitated the competitor's point of view on any given topic.

Use Target Keywords Where They Matter Most

To send search engines strong signals about the intent of your content, it is vital that you use your target keywords in the following places (prioritized by importance and explained further below):

- Title tag; the title or headline of your article
- Headline tags (your subtopics)
- Meta description
- Internal links within content and the Alt attribute of images

Internal linking and alt text for images are more granular SEO elements and the publisher will often take care of these. But to gain even more ground as an in-demand freelance writer, learn about optimizing internal links and alt attributes for images and provide these with your work. You will save the publisher time.

The Title Tag: Still the Most Powerful Element

The title tag gives the search engine the main title or headline of your online article (page, blog post, etc.). This is presented in search engines and the web browser as the title of a website page or article, and it is one of the strongest indicators to search engines of what that page is about.

If you are creating page copy for the homepage of a website, a best practice is to target three of the most important keywords that describe that business or website.

Make sure your target keywords are part of your title tag, placed as near to the beginning as possible.

For example, if you created a page about learning how to write for SEO and your target keyword was "writing for SEO" (which has a search volume of 1,600 per month as per SEMrush, May 2020), you'll want that target keyword or a close variation of it as near to the front of the title as possible.

An optimized title tag for this example could be, "Writing Tips for SEO: From Keywords to Meta Descriptions." Remember that title tags should be about 60 characters (not words). The above example is 56 characters.

Put as much time into getting your title right as you spend actually creating content.

When creating your titles, always think in terms of simplicity first. As author of *Building a StoryBrand: Clarify Your Message So Customers Will Listen* Don Miller says, creative and cute don't sell. Title tags are the first step towards selling to your audience. Speak the language of your target audience.

Don't Forget the Meta Description!

Too many people miss out on the opportunity to customize meta descriptions, and it is a vital process for engaging your audience in search.

The meta description is that little snippet of copy underneath the title in a search result. They are typically 150-160 characters (again, not words!); any longer may be truncated by search engines.

Every page on your website should have a customized one. If not, the search engines will auto-generate them, and the auto-generated meta description may not help influence the searchers to click the link and visit your work of writing.

Google says that meta descriptions do not influence search rankings, but there are many factors that affect rankings indirectly.

If a meta description supports the title and further adds to curiosity, the click-through rate will be higher and *that* is an impactful SEO ranking factor.

Use your main keyword from the title in your meta description. When a searcher queries that keyword, it will be bold in your meta description, further influencing a click to your article.

Get creative with your meta descriptions. As Julia McCoy says in her must-read book for modern writers, *So You Think You Can Write? The Definitive Guide to Successful Online Writing*, "treat meta descriptions as free ad copy for your website pages."

Header Tags (or Simply Subheadings)

Header tags are as important for SEO as they are for UX (user experience). These are subtopics that nicely divide your article into sections readers can quickly skim.

Write your subheadings so that they garner attention but also incorporate your target keyword(s). This helps with SEO. When tagged as a "header" or "H" tag, you are telling search engines that these carry much importance.

There are headline 1 (H1), headline 2 (H2), headline 3 (H3) tags and so forth, and each one typically gets smaller in design. I typically don't go past a headline 3 tag, though I'll occasionally use a headline 4 tag. Just look at the sizes.

Use just one H1 tag—this should be your main title. Throughout the article, stick with H2 or H3 tags as the title of each subsection.

Use Bold & Bullet Points Wherever Possible

Google pays attention to these, including when awarding featured snippets (those first-seen boxes of information for various search queries). Make sure to use target keywords in bold and bullet points when possible.

If a section of content can be laid out in bullet points, use them. These, along with bolded words, send additional signals to search engines about the value you place on that content.

From a user perspective, these "BBs" garner quick attention. Bullet points help organize the content for easier reading, and bold words quickly draw attention to that section, helping the reader understand what you think is important.

More on Internal Links

Internal links throughout your copy are vital for SEO because they show relationships to other content across your website.

External links to trusted sources also provide more authority to your article, helping the rankings. Make sure each "anchor text" is optimized; this is simply the word or phrase that you link from.

More on Optimizing Images

Search engines can't read images, which is why each one needs an Alt Text (alternative text) tag.

This provides a textual description of the image and is also an important accessibility feature.

Use captions where necessary and always give images a custom title before uploading, making sure to use your target keywords.

Always compress images (reduce the file size) to improve loading times and overall page speed.

In today's world of endless online content options for search engines and readers, strong content writing combined with SEO is a must. Neither stands well on its own.

Now, let's get to some topic and content strategy tips.

CHAPTER 7

CREATING BLOG STRATEGIES: 3 STEPS TO TAKE AND 4 TO AVOID

This chapter is dedicated to those freelance and agency writers who need help creating content strategies for their clients, with a focus on blogs.

The power of consistent and frequent blogging is immeasurable.

Too many businesses fail to understand the power of blogging or take a haphazard approach, moving along as either budget or resources become available. This creates a massive opportunity for those that make it a priority.

In reality, blogging can be one the largest producers of qualified leads and ultimately ROI.

You need a strategy to truly benefit from everything a blog has to offer and the deal strategy begins with three specific steps and four mistakes to avoid. (The mistakes are especially important; these are lessons I've learned in over a decade of working with blogs, both as a writer/strategist and now an agency owner with clients who rely on blogs for sales and increased revenue. Learn from my mistakes to save yourself time, money, and frustration!)

Content creation is the focus of every one of my agency's overall SEO strategies and blogs are the pillars on which all other efforts stand.

A blog provides:

- Stronger SEO due to more content and more keywords
- Newsletter content for building loyalty from existing clients on the email list
- Fuel for social media to provide value to audience/followers
- Link building through natural shares of strong content and reach-out campaigns

The tactics discussed in this chapter have worked for a multiple of my clients in the past. Don't mistake this for a cookie-cutter approach; each client has a unique audience and services or products.

Even two direct competitors require different content strategies based on their positioning within the market.

When modern writers expand the value of their service offerings by learning SEO or learning how to create ROI-producing blog strategies, demand for their work increases. I know many freelancers who are also tasked with creating blog strategies for their clients.

First and foremost, you want to have a discussion about the client's end goals. Is it their mission to build value over a 10-year period and retain customers (think of a plastic surgeon or investment company)?

Or is the mission to highlight products to one-time buyers (think of a DNA test business)?

These two goals require completely different strategies. Understanding the end goal puts you in position to take these next three important steps.

Step 1: "Intentional SEO Storytelling" Strategy

SEO combined with intentional storytelling is the basis of my agency's successful blogging strategies. Many others focus on only the SEO side of things; on creating blog content based on keywords and the searcher's intent (their intended outcome).

But you should start with this type of keyword research built around a searcher's intent. Remember, this strategy has the greatest impact when the client's technical SEO is strong, and the website is structured around a strong keyword mapping strategy.

The latter simply means that the client's website is targeting the correct keywords for the correct service pages - such as a main category page of products directed towards one type (Ducati Monster motorcycle parts) or an educational page about a certain element (Ducati Monster model history).

With technical and mapping aspects correct, you can begin your keyword research for blogging around a searcher's intent.

Let me explain.

Yoast, a genius tool for WordPress users, mentions four types of intent :

- Educational/informational: People search for "What is the history of a Ducati Monster?"
- Navigational: People search for "Ducati North America"
- Transactional: People search for "Ducati Monsters for Sale"
- Commercial Investigation Intent: People search for information to help them understand what they're buying; "Ducati Monster problems"

For blogging purposes, educational/informational and commercial investigation are typically the driving factors behind keyword research.

With this intent in mind, I begin generating a list of long-tail keywords for our blogs. I typically end up with a list of around 100 long-tail keywords to initially focus on. These long-tail keywords usually have lower search volumes, making it much easier to rank content for them higher in the search results.

Many SEOs I've worked with would ignore keywords with less than 70 or so searches per month. Depending on how lucrative the outcome, I sometimes go as low as 10. If your business sells a

$10,000 coaching service, those 10 people are vital for success.

Now, think like a journalist asking questions. Talk to the client and focus on the top ROI services/products for that moment. Also ask if they are planning any product/service launches or promotions.

This can guide some blog topics; you want to start seeding the audience and a blog is the perfect platform to do so.

Once you have generated these terms and a list of topics related to your top ROI services/products, launches, and/or promotions, search Google for them and analyze the results.

I also check Reddit, Quora, and the typical social media channels like Facebook and Instagram to see what questions people are asking about subjects related to those terms. And never forget about the snippet box of questions on Google.

With that information listed on a clean spreadsheet, I then look at some competitor rankings for those keywords using tools like SEMrush.

This helps us find other keywords related to the list of keywords we have already generated, and to find additional opportunities.

Never simply analyze the number 1-3 spots on Google and simply attempt to write a better article. Even if it's in your subconscious, you may simply mimic what the others are saying, adding to the digital noise.

As I mentioned in the previous chapter on SEO, only check competitors for keyword opportunities—never copy their actual content. Writers should have a deep knowledge of the competitive landscape. But take warning - nothing should be replicated unless you're in the breaking news industry where stories will naturally repeat.

Then there's the story. Most forget to add the storytelling element, but it is vital for cutting through the noise.

For example, a storyline in this chapter is about how there is no cookie-cutter blog strategy for every client.

Step 2: USP-Focused Strategy

It's time to focus on what makes your client's services or products truly stand out in their industry.

The more niche, the easier it is to focus on your unique selling position (USP)—that thing that makes you "remarkable."

If you are creating an SEO-blogging strategy for a client who only sells Ducati Monster motorcycle parts, finding your USP is going to be fairly simple. However, if you're marketing *all* Ducati parts, you have a much more difficult task ahead.

Your USP cannot be something generic, such as "100-percent guarantee" or "quickest delivery" or "cheapest prices." That's what everyone will do, and it doesn't show one ounce of uniqueness.

What if you not only sold the part, but had educational resources on how to install those parts via video or from an official technical manual?

What if you had service technicians on-hand to answer questions, or affiliates with the client's closest and most reputable Ducati techs?

That is something unique. And that needs to be highlighted in your blogging efforts.

For example, one of ContentMender's USPs is helping clients define and refine their USPs, and then creating SEO and content strategies that help exploit those USPs.

Back to the Ducati part's dealer example. Though your business may be a parts-selling business, you can now blog about the top qualities of a Ducati service rep. What questions should you ask? Do they use OEM or aftermarket parts, and which are better?

This strategy helps you become a valuable source of information for the do-it-yourselfers. They may not be searching for a part at that moment, but you will be, as author John Hall says, "Top of Mind" when the sales opportunity occurs later on.

This also helps you rank for longer-tail keywords related to your products or services that you wouldn't have focused on, had you not first created your USP and exploited it through blogging. This will help your overall rankings and brand authority.

Step 3: Sales Blending

It's time to create a content calendar, and this is where the sales team becomes a powerful tool in your content strategy.

Bloggers should work closely with the sales team. This is crucial in understanding a business's true audience.

First, understand that the idea of a "sales funnel" is dead. Rather, transform your thinking to think of it as a cyclone, a concept Eric Keiles and Mike Lieberman shared in *Smash the Funnel: The Cyclonic Buyer Journey.*

Read that book. It'll change your perspective on sales.

For now, know that eight "cyclones" are present in the customer-centric model that revolves around customer service, marketing and sales:

- Pre-Awareness
- Awareness
- Education
- Consideration
- Evaluation
- Rationalization
- Decision Making
- Ongoing Delivery

The goal is to create content that educates the audience across these various cyclones.

Most of my agency's client blog campaigns reflect the following:

- 50% written for newbies. They are just learning about your business, industry, products, or services. These are the types of people you want to continually feed valuable information so they remember you when they're ready to make a purchase. They are beginning their journey and researching from square one.
- 25% for intermediate. They are educated and seeking more granular information. Here's where you can provide expert-level information to showcase your knowledge and build authority.
- 25% for experts. They are extremely knowledgeable. These are the readers who are looking for expert opinion to scale their knowledge. They are also looking for the optimal partner to help scale their business. This is amazing for what I call "natural networking;" when an expert from another business notices strong and unique content around their areas of expertise, they'll reach out. It has happened to me for multiple blogging clients due to articles I wrote in other leading digital marketing publications.

Here's a quick example from the ContentMender blog:

- 50% of the blogs published are for those just learning about content creation and SEO.

- 25% are for those who understand content creation and SEO, but are searching for reputable help.
- 25% are for the experts, who are typically CMOs or SEO managers that are looking for immediate partners.

You can add value to anyone within any portion of the sales cyclone. This tactic doesn't work for everyone; a medical peer-to-peer publication, for example, wants only expert-level content. But for the majority of businesses, practices, and self-promoting websites (authors, musicians), this sales blend is optimal.

Through this content, you can nurture customers from the very beginning of their journey, where they are asking simple, informational questions. As customers become educated and smarter, they look to the source of this knowledge and become clients.

And Here's What NOT to DO

This simple, 3-step strategy has worked for many of my agency's clients, from Bridgestone to a local pest company to a self-directed IRA business. Now, avoid these four blog strategy mistakes that can sabotage your best efforts.

Mistake #1: Not Performing 3 Layers of Research

Three types of research should be performed before a single word is typed:

- Overall market analysis
- Target audience analysis
- Traditional competitive research

Overall Market Analysis

This gives you an overall snapshot of your market including its size, profitability, distribution channels, trends, and growth rate. This doesn't need to take a crazy amount of energy or resources—it's just good to know what the big picture is across the industry.

Do a quick search of "(industry) market analysis (current year)", and you'll find loads of reputable sources to create a snapshot of this information. The data can also be used in blogs for research, so make sure all the research is fresh.

Target Audience Analysis

First, get a few crucial questions answered by the CEO, CMO, sales, customer service, etc. You are looking for various perspectives as to who the target audience is and what characteristics define them.

You can help the business further refine their target audience, and provide more value than the blog itself.

- What questions are they asking online (forums, social media, etc.)?
- What is their income range?
- What are their buying habits?
- What services or products are they using that you can replace and do better?

These insights can help you identify potentially impactful topics you may not have explored otherwise. (Even just typing niche-specific keywords into Reddit or Quora will show you loads of questions your target audience is asking.)

Your goal is to answer those questions with a personality specific to your brand.

Traditional Competitive Research

Competitive research is the third layer of your blog strategy research. Here, you take snapshots of exactly what your closest competitors are doing:

- What topics are they exploring?
- How often are they posting?
- What keywords are they ranking for?
- What is their overall website strategy (traffic, top-ranking blogs, CTA usage, paid advertising ads and spend, etc.)?

I typically look at 10 competitors: five directly from the business leaders who say who their top competitors are, and five from SEO tools that show who the top competitors are from an SEO perspective.

Remember, competitive research is just for insight, not repeating. Just because one blog topic is working for a competitor doesn't mean it'll work for your business or client. I like to use competitive research to identify keywords I want to focus on, and to see what I can do better.

These three levels of data compiled can be used as a baseline by which you'll measure progress going forward.

Be sure to include a snapshot of your starting point. Company leaders will want to see metrics such as increased traffic, or rankings for broad keywords that are sometimes impossible to rank for.

It's the agency or blogger's responsibility to be a guide and educator. Explain the importance of quality over quantity and showcase metrics such as rankings for keywords that are actually converting, instead.

Help them understand the long-term value of your SEO and blogging strategy.

I tell clients that true results won't become apparent until 6-12 months of consistent blogging. Though results may come in much quicker, it's always good to over-deliver versus overpromising.

Mistake #2: Not Thinking of Frequency and Consistency

In the world of blogging, frequency and consistency are key. This goes for your content calendar and publishing times to the consistency of voice, tone, and style across all of your client's blogs.

Sure, you may be speaking to three different target audiences in various stages of the sales funnel (as explained in sales blending above in my "3 To-Dos" list), but your voice, tone, and style should be united across each blog.

Voice and tone are contingent on each brand. If the tone is laid back, stick with that style across each blog.

Keep the same voice and tone for all content on the website, social media, and newsletters to show consistency across the brand.

As for style, do you write in short, choppy sentences? Do you adhere to AP or APA styling? Do you write many listicles, and stick to the same format each time such as numbering conventions for each point? Do you mention #1 or the final number first?

These are all things to ask yourself. It doesn't matter what your tone or style of writing is, as long as it's consistent.

Mistake #3: Writing Without SEO Guidelines on a Technically Sound Platform

Before I work with a client, I run a quick SEO audit of their website. If they are missing vital elements such as speed, title tags, or unique meta descriptions, I recommend completing a deeper technical SEO audit first to address those main issues.

Consider this: you want to change out the tires on your car to improve your ride. If you don't have an engine, what's the point?

You need to get to the mechanic first so they can fix that problem first. Same for a deeper technical SEO audit. A blog strategy can't reach its full potential if that foundation of technical SEO bits is not in place.

All blogs must also be written with SEO in mind. After I complete the necessary research and create the strategy and blog calendar, I provide my writers with "SEO Content Templates," which are basically guidelines that ensure the optimized headline, target keyword, all related keywords needed for user intent and semantic latent indexing, and a list of the top URLs for research are part of the writing process for each piece.

Mistake #4: Forgetting About a Strong Editorial Process

This is huge. You can have the most optimized platform, unique blog posts, and consistent voice in the world, but if your grammar is sloppy or information not factually correct, your prospective clients will go elsewhere—and quickly.

I use a seven-layer blog creation process that blends in best practices of grammar, style, fact-checking, and SEO, something I reviewed in the "Learn to Deal with a Process that is Controlled by Editors" section of Chapter 5.

The process begins with individual keyword research and SEO guidelines that have optimized titles that adhere to an overall blog-calendar strategy.

Once the first draft comes in, it goes through factual edits, then another round for grammar/style.

Then there's a third edit of SEO elements and creation of a "plug n' play" document that I provide to clients if they upload to the CMS in-house.

Even then, I ask clients to allow my agency to perform one more edit in preview mode on their website before the piece goes live.

The preview environment changes quickly from Google Doc or Word to the actual website. This tactic allows you to edit the blog with fresh eyes, exactly as it will appear to readers.

There are hundreds of ways to create a blog strategy, but I know these work. I use the above process as a starting point for every client. After a few months or quarters of testing, I may find valuable additions such as focusing on CEOs who have a strong personal brand and capitalizing on it by making them the focus of blogs or authors of the blogs.

Test. Evaluate. Remain the course or pivot, depending on what your results tell you. Optimizing a blog strategy is a lifelong client process that's cyclical.

And remember to always tell a story.

Next, it's time to amplify those blogs (or any other online content you create).

Chapter 8

Amplify Content Through Various Social Media Channels

I hope you understand by now that all writing, from email to blogs to books, is a process, not an end product.

My process is influenced by the many lessons from Don Murray's style of prewriting, writing, and rewriting—or, as he calls it, prevision, vision, and revision. For the modern digital writer, though, there is more to this process.

In the digital space, we also must focus on amplifying what we create through whatever digital channels we can, from social media to personal websites to shares from other reputable authors/publications.

Your amplification process could involve guest blogging on popular websites, to add value to that website's readers while simultaneously building your personal brand as a writer.

Yes, a writer's life is 80% experience and 20% writing, but it doesn't stop there. To be heard in noisy digital spaces today, you need to give it 110%.

I spend countless hours creating content for my business blog at ContentMender. One blog post that many of my writing friends have found valuable is *7 Time Management Tips for Online Writers (Proactive > Reactive).*[6].

After floating around the search engines for a week, it had been read about 300 times with the average visitor reading for just over four minutes.

When I published it to my personal and ContentMender channels, it reached over 1,500 people in six days and the average read time grew to just under eight minutes.

That was pretty decent for a relatively unknown website offering lessons in time management for other writers. At the time, my business website and domain were just a few months old. As SEOs understand, "young" websites have no authority due to a lack of links and content—and no authority equates to crappy search results.

Months later, I started writing for *Forbes* as an unpaid guest writer. An article I wrote about time management in early 2019 reached 500 readers on the first day, then 5,000 within a week.

---

[6] https://contentmender.com/7-time-management-tips-for-content-writers-proactive-reactive/

Another piece I wrote more recently on the basics of SEO reached 27,000 readers in just two weeks.

That's a lot of views. The link in my bio sends readers to ContentMender's blog, where views of my other articles on time management and writing jumped 25%.

The power of guest posting—especially for reputable publications like *Forbes* and *Search Engine Journal*—helped amplify my messages across all my writing. It also helped build my brand; when I wrote this book, I knew I already had an audience for it.

Now, I'm no authority on social media. I don't pay much attention to "vanity metrics" such as likes or shares.

But I know that participating in social works. It is a must for the 21st Century writer (especially those who freelance for various publications/blogs for a living). Those publications want to see that you can draw an audience, and social media is a great way to do that.

You can also use social to promote client work; just be careful if you're a ghostwriter or have signed a non-disclosure agreement with certain people or businesses.

The more you share and amplify, the more they will benefit, and the more work you'll have. It's the same principle as writing with SEO in mind—your writing will stand out in search results and draw more readers. Social shares have the added benefit of positively impacting search rankings, even if only indirectly.

I won't lie... sometimes I get extremely lazy with social media. But it's part of modern life and, when used wisely, a powerful tool to amplify your writing and keep you working and sharing your message (whatever that message may be).

Here are a few tips to get you started on various platforms.

Facebook

There are nearly 8 billion people on earth and 1 billion of those people are on Facebook. Users span every country, demographic, and generation.

This is an obvious channel for promoting your writing, whether personal or for clients. Don't just share the link to your content, though. Write a message or pull a strong quote from the blog. I use the meta description—the 160-character description that markets that blog in search results—since that work is already completed. Add hashtags and make sure you tag any professional or business mentioned in the blog. You might be surprised at who will share your work.

Always respond to private messages or comments on your posts. Even the negative ones. People air their thoughts constantly across social media.

Each comment is an opportunity to engage a reader and even rethink your message. Communicate, build a conversation, and learn from your social audience.

Have your scribble tablet next to you while reading these so you can take notes. Those notes may one day turn into a new blog, as has happened for me many times in my writing for the motorcycle industry.

Want to make an even bigger impact? "Boost" a post by paying for it to reach a wider audience. This tactic especially works for listicles and value-driven content that is needed to get your personal or client readers into the sales funnel.

Twitter

Twitter is a great place to amplify content. Create something snappy that drives curiosity in those 280 characters.

As with Facebook, make sure you use one or two hashtags and tag any respective professionals or companies mentioned within your blogs to help you get shares. Always respond and be part of the conversation.

Instagram

Though Instagram is photo-centric, you can still get traction for your blog by building your branding here. Post a picture from the blog and link to it from your bio page.

Tag anyone mentioned and use hashtags (you can use a lot more hashtags on Instagram than on Facebook or Twitter, as it's more "socially acceptable" to use 10 or 20 at a time without appearing spammy). Build that conversation and learn from your readers.

LinkedIn

LinkedIn is where serious shares happen, especially for B2B content. The genius of LinkedIn is you can tap into the exact audience you want on a serious level, from CEOs to authors to those who influence.

One of my favorites to follow is Simon Sinek. He is seriously active on LinkedIn, and his ROI from sharing his content across the channel must escalate quickly - if not, why would he waste his time?

You can use hashtags here, too.

You have the option to write original content and publish to LinkedIn as an article. However, I prefer to own the content on my own blog, so I stay away from this.

Even so, you can curate your blogs on LinkedIn channels by writing a unique summary, providing a strong quote from the article, and linking to the original source. Once again, tag anyone mentioned.

Medium

Medium is a blogging platform with a built-in audience. Be careful here if you own a website or are sharing content you have created for clients. Simply copy and pasting a full blog post on

Medium is a no-no in the world of SEO as only one version of any piece of content—the original—will appear in search. If you want to republish content to Medium, make sure you list and link to the original source from the version on Medium.

If your goal is more brand-building than SEO, reposting on Medium can help you achieve more eyes and more shares. When not marketing actual products or services for a business, sometimes this duplicate content issue may be worth it.

Or, create original content for Medium and link back to one of your blogs as a reference. This is the perfect way to expose your content while giving you the extra practice in the process of writing. You can never write enough.

Reddit

Remember our talks about meta descriptions in Chapter 6 about SEO? Reddit explains itself well in its meta description: "Reddit is a network of communities based on people's interests. Find communities you're interested in, and become part of an online community!"

Reddit is a place where questions and answers happen.

Find a Reddit based around your industry or subject and engage with the community. Once you have built a bit of credibility, feel free to share links to your work—again, personal or client work.

Don't just force the links. Wait and build respect with other readers before sharing your work and make sure that you participate and engage more than you promote.

Quora

Quora is another place like Reddit, and has a strong meta description to explain just what it does: "Quora is a place to gain and share knowledge. It's a platform to ask questions and connect with people who contribute unique insights and quality answers."

The process is the same as Reddit. Become respected, then share your valuable blog work while adding valuable information.

Can I stress valuable enough?

Guest Blogging

Guest blogging is my favorite amplification tactic for both personal brand and client content. Guest blogging has helped me land clients and loyal readers for my own blogs and for clients alike.

Most publications won't allow you to simply discuss or link to a personal blog, but a link to your blog or website's homepage in your bio is typical.

Only publish your guest posts to popular, authoritative blogs. Your time is limited (remember that 80/20 mindset!).

PR Efforts

Find reputable publications and authors/ journalists to be part of your network. Reach out to them in an *authentic* manner to offer any assistance they need for resources.

What does authenticity mean in PR? It means that you don't spam strangers with cold emails and vague pitches such as, "To whom it concerns, I think my article will add awesome value to your publication."

You need to create a relationship with those publications or writers first. A good introduction often occurs via commenting on their blogs and social media posts.

Do your research. Know the names and direct emails of the people you want to pitch. If you have a relationship with an acquaintance of that person or someone within the publication or business, let them know.

HARO

HARO stands for "Help A Reporter Out." I've used this platform for the past decade, first as a publication representative asking others for help with an article, then as a source for other reporters needing valuable information. Using this journalism tool has led to serious mentions for my company and client brands.

When you or your client are mentioned in a publication, the author typically includes a link back to your website, which is a valuable SEO signal.

This HARO work was so powerful that my agency turned it into a service offering for brand building PR and SEO. We answer HARO Q&As on behalf of the client.

Ask for Links in Other Articles

When you read an article that could have benefitted from your tip or perspective, pitch the publication, writer, editor, or web developer.

Keep it short and simple, and point them to the link you want them to use. Let them decide. Don't follow up and be annoying. Like I said above, be *authentic*.

Ask Friends/Family/Employees to Share Via Social

Sometimes we overlook the simplest engagement methods. Ask your friends, family, business associates, and employees to share your blogs.

Expose on YOUR Website

This is for freelancers who own websites, businesses, or publications.

Remember, when you publish on Medium or LinkedIn, you don't own that content. Those platforms may reach millions more, but can change their business model in seconds and you lose all that hard work.

Write the majority of your original work for your own website, and amplify it using these platforms.

Don't host on a free blog platform (eg.: mysite.wordpress.com), but on your own hosting and domain, eg.: mysite.com.

There are other blogging platforms out there, but WordPress is affordable, easy to optimize, and simple to use. Plus it's easy to optimize for search engines.

Newsletters

If you own your own website, make sure all the articles you create are shared to subscribers in an email newsletter.

Many business owners and bloggers miss out on the opportunity to re-engage existing readers because they don't do the work of curating posts in a newsletter.

An owned newsletter list is a warm, interested audience. Continually feed them so you stay, as John Hall would say, "Top of Mind."

Some Final Thoughts

If you're dedicated to getting the most impact from your personal and/or client work, you should also be dedicated to amplifying the work through various channels.

Social sharing is powerful—even more so when your writing resonates and people are inspired to reshare on their own.

But you have to get it in front of them first. The amplification tactics you've learned in this chapter will help you establish that all-important TAR: trust, authority, and reputation.

For those with clients, this sharing shows that you value the client. It helps strengthen the relationship between you and that client. The exception to sharing, of course, is when you've signed a nondisclosure agreement.

Let's get back to this beautiful process of writing with some helpful things I've discovered around madness, biohacking, and relaxing.

Chapter 9

Optimize Your 'Creative Spend'

Writing sometimes writes itself, and the direction can change quickly.

For example, when I sat down to start writing "11 Habits of Content Creators Who Optimize 'Creative Spend'" for *Search Engine Journal,*[7] the concept was actually, "what writers can learn from biohackers." But once I began writing, the subject matter transformed.

The greatest content creators and writers know how to optimize what I call "creative spend," which is measured in creative units, or CUs. The idea was borrowed from the motorcycle-racing trainer and founder of Yamaha Champions Riding School Nick Ienatsch's "100 Points of Grip" theory.[8]

Basically, every motorcyclist has 100 points of traction when a motorcycle is straight up and

---

[7] https://www.searchenginejournal.com/11-habits-of-content-creators-who-optimize-creative-spend/299863/
[8] https://www.youtube.com/watch?v=Fy1AIAc76Qo

down. But when you put various inputs in such as leaning the motorcycle, braking, or using the throttle, you lose various points of grip.

The more grip, the faster and safer you can ride. But when you start taking away points of grip, such as 30 due to braking and 20 while leaning, you're only at 50 points of grip. You can now crash much easier.

The same principle applies to CUs for the writers' creative process.

Visualize one of those old-school wooden rulers used in elementary schools. Picture it having 100 creative units. At 100, your creative energy is at its peak and you complete high-quality work in less time. At 0 CUs, your creative energy is depleted. Here, the work is unacceptable and takes much more time and energy to complete

For simplicity, say the average writer can finish work at around 50 CUs. The writing here is average; it's stale, boring, and dull. It's been written just to say it's finished and nothing has been done to scale their writing. We'll say that anything below 50 is a fail—an incomplete.

Ideally, you want to keep your CUs as close to 100 as possible, and certainly well above 50. The longer you remain there, in that highly creative space, the higher quality work you'll complete—and more of it— with less effort. Optimizing your creative spend gives you back a bit of the only thing you could never get back: your time.

Once you achieve your optimal creative energy, how do you stay hypercharged all day?

Writers need to nurture daily habits that recharge those CUs and replace the negative habits that rob your CUs inventory.

In Chapter 4, I talked about optimizing time and how the smallest things, like replying to a social media post or an email, may seem unharmful at the time. But these constant interruptions deplete a writer's creative units.

Say you are on Facebook just before you are supposed to start a project that requires much creative energy, for example. You were fully charged with 100 CUs, but lost 30 debating with someone about a piece of information shared.

The exchange was annoying or made you angry; some emotion was invoked and expended. You're reduced to 70 units of creativity and you haven't even started writing yet.

You will complete the work, but not in the best possible way. And this is just one example; all day long we face distractions from co-workers, family, news and other media, daydreaming, life insurance telemarketers, and more.

You need to optimize your creative spend to create only the best content in the least amount of time. You do this in two ways: either you do things that recharge your creativity, or you avoid depleting them in the first place. Ideally, you're going to do both.

Here are a few habits that great writers utilize to always work at the top range of their creative output. You'll recognize some from previous chapters as I underscore again what is most important.

Prioritize Physical Health Habits

If you don't feel your best, you won't create your best content. I lived a bulk of my early 20s as a musician and want-to-be fiction novelist, spending serious time in barrooms thick with smoke and a drink always near.

I also only slept for about three hours each night. I was never overweight or sick but, looking back, my full potential was never within reach. My CUs were depleted through many fun but ultimately unproductive activities.

A nervous breakdown in my late 20s was the proverbial wake-up call. Health became a priority, and even more so when I launched my agency.

Nowadays if I don't perform at my best, my businesses fail. If that's not an incentive to keep my physical and mental fitness top of mind, I don't know what would be. You need to find your motivation.

Physical fitness is simple, so long as you don't have underlying health conditions. Eat well and exercise. Mental fitness is more challenging, especially for content creators who must consistently perform near those 100 CUs daily to achieve true success.

For writers, mental fitness is not only mental wellness, but also the ability to focus and maintain clarity. Physical fitness can be a great help here, too.

Sure, some unfit writers are brilliant. But when you are physically fit, that balance becomes easier to achieve. You sleep well and wake refreshed.

You don't have aching muscles or the chronic pain of poor posture and excess weight distracting you from your work. Physical fitness is part of your distraction-free zone, which we'll expand upon in this next point.

Design a Distraction-Free Zone for Deep Focus

During creative hours, make it a habit to give yourself distraction-free time that will keep your CUs high and allow your mind to get into a super deep focus.

In order to be truly distraction-free, don't check emails, text messages, social media feeds, etc. Make this a habit and your content will skyrocket in both quantity and quality.

This can be challenging, as many writers work on a computer with their phone nearby. Turn off all notifications on your laptop, phone, and any other nearby electronic devices. Work in just one screen or browser window.

For deep focus, anything that may cause distractions must be turned off.

Let co-workers and/or your boss know when you're in your distraction-free mode. Email and social media are certainly the biggest culprits of sucking up precious creative units, but office distractions are definitely the next.

The amount of time you spend in your distraction-free zone brings us to the next habit.

Find Your Creative Time Limit and Habitually Return to It

The next question is, how long should you spend in your distraction-free creative time zone? This varies for every content creator (and for some, the time may vary on a project-by-project basis).

For example, if I'm writing about business, self-development, writing, or motorcycles, I can write at my creative peak for up to three hours.

But if I'm creating content strategies or editing blogs for clients, sometimes my maximum time for peak performance is around 90 minutes.

This doesn't mean you only have three hours or 90 minutes of peak creativity during any given day. It means you need to replenish your CUs by doing something else for a certain amount of time.

This may be a 15-minute walk around the block, a non-digital reading session, washing dishes, or cutting down a tree. The task doesn't matter; what matters is that you get your mind off what you're doing for a quick recharge.

For some, it may be tough to completely replenish their CUs and they may only get one extra period of high energy to work on their project.

How often you can replenish your CUs each day depends solely on your approach. If you remain distraction-free and are feeling good, you can do this all day.

If not, don't worry. The more you make it a habit to recharge your CUs throughout the day, the more periods of creative energy you'll have to finish your content projects.

Like all good habits, this becomes easier and more effective in time and with regular practice.

Organize Time Every Week for Projects

Don't wait for those proverbial creative juices to start flowing or that muse of yours to show up.

Consistently block time into your calendar for writing, whether your workflow requires that you do this every day or every week.

Initiate your creativity daily. Don't wait for a creative awakening.

As E.B White says, "A writer who waits for ideal conditions under which to work will die without putting a word on paper."

Try to Accomplish the Most Creative Tasks Early

After a great night's sleep, the mind is fresh. This is when you can truly take advantage of your most creative units.

On my "creative" days (say, when I need to edit a final draft of something important) I refuse to check email, social media, or even my phone until all my creative work is complete. This sometimes goes through 3 p.m., even if I'm up at my usual 6:30 a.m. to start work.

As you can imagine, this helps me stay *super* refreshed because you can't worry about the things you don't know about.

I say "Try" to accomplish your creative tasks early in the subheading above because some people still have other times when their creativity is highest and that is okay, too. I used to find my peak creativity from 11 p.m. through whenever I went to sleep.

But after starting my own business, priorities changed and so did my mind's freshest times (largely due to the healthier habits I developed, such as a strict sleep schedule, dieting, and biohacking).

Another tactic I use is working after short naps. Einstein was the king of naps, and his creativity was obviously high at all times. Winston Churchill and Salvador Dali also knapped religiously. I sometimes take 15-to-20-minute energizing naps before I have to create new content so I can bring the freshest perspective to my desk.

I still do some late-night work, but don't like the impact it has on my sleeping patterns. Again, these are all rituals I've nurtured to create habits that help me to capitalize on my creativity while optimizing my health and life. You need to find what works for you.

Slow the Mind Drastically Before A Project

This is a hack I use over and over for projects that begin in the middle of the day. Midday meetings and the unexpected tasks that pop up can leave writers feeling drained. You might feel that the day has become a waste.

You need a hack to slow the mind drastically before starting or continuing that next project, to supercharge your creative units.

If I know something is going to use nearly all of my creative spend for that day, such as back-to-back client meetings, I'll spend an hour or so doing something that has absolutely nothing to do with my upcoming project.

Make it something you enjoy doing; a down-time that can shake your mind off the project in a second. Maybe it's a hike or jog around town, or a break for video games or cooking. It doesn't matter what the downtime is.

My personal favorites are a hot bath while reading, a fast motorcycle ride, or a blues guitar jam session.

Also, consider your time limits. An hour or recharging works perfectly for me and I can then head into my creative zone with complete energy, getting much higher quality work completed in less time.

Others may need more or less time; find what works best for you. If you discover that these simple acts of enjoyable downtime build more energy for your project, keep it going and turn that ritual into a habit.

Don't Give Writer's Block Any Credence; It's a BS Delusion

I've written about this numerous times for many publications and will say it again: writer's block is pure BS.

People who say they have writer's block either:

- Aren't equipping themselves with a healthy lifestyle conducive to writing,
- Are not capitalizing on their most creative times to write and bringing creative units to the table,
- Or are just plain lazy.

I'd argue that laziness is most often the main culprit of writer's block, and laziness is a primary outcome of depleted creative units. Make it a habit to deny the existence of writer's block as some outside force or phenomenon that's holding you back. The only issue you have is a lack of CUs.

That's it.

Just Start Writing

Sometimes all of the energy you need is there, your CUs are maximized, and the words still just won't flow. In this case, make it your go-to habit to simply start writing about anything even remotely related to the subject. Just get those fingers moving.

Write what you already know. This is the easiest place to start. Don't worry how sloppy this is, just get your thoughts flowing.

Sometimes it only takes the physical movement of the fingers on the keyboard to get your words flowing.

From there, ideas begin to take shape. Unless you're a novelist, don't go all Kerouac and continue writing in this stream-of-conscious style. Once you get going, you can begin to crystallize your thoughts and write more cleanly.

Strong writing—the type you get paid to do—requires the consideration of both user experience and search purposes. That takes us to the next habit of great content creators.

Outline, Write, Edit, and Edit Again

This is a simple process that writers have used for centuries. When you outline a piece of writing, you are forced to organize the information in smaller chunks. You can then easily arrange them into the most coherent layout.

In one quick search, you'll find multiple ways to outline any type of writing, from fiction novels to essays. But let's focus on the type of writing millions of authors and businesses are doing every day: blog-style articles.

This basic outline works well for me:

- Working Title

- Subheading Titles
- Intro (2-3 main points)
- 2-3 main points under each subheading
- Conclusion (2-3 main points)

Sometimes I write a conclusion and support it with sub-headings before writing the title (hence why it's a "working title") and intro, and sometimes I do things the exact opposite. It all depends on my prior knowledge of the subject and what I learn as I begin my research.

This outlining process also plays into your SEO strategy. Those subheadings turn into headline tags where you can further insert important keywords, and it helps to organize the information for search engines.

Spend as much creative energy on this outline as you do on the writing itself. Once the first draft is complete, it's time to edit. And edit again. And again if necessary.

Always approach the final edit after at least a full day away from the subject, and complete the final edit when your creative units are at their peak.

For me, this is early in the morning on my "creative" days, and I don't check email, news, or my phone until I have completed my final edits.

On larger projects—that is, anything over 1,000 words— make sure you get your hands and eyes on printed hard copies.

Don't forget to change the document from landscape back to portrait so you can save time on editing. A print-out in landscape will be a horizontal page, versus the standard vertical page.

If you can edit on horizontal hard copies, do it. I can't; it's a psychological element of embracing the familiarity of standard print outs.

Read Daily, Including Every Book on Writing

This is worth repeating once again for the impact it has on your creative process.

If you want to write well, you must read.

Make it a habit to read daily. Audiobooks and podcasts also work, but I'm a sucker for marking up margins and collecting those books for future reference.

The more you read, the more you'll absorb all the elements of good writing—the syntax, voice, structure, and more. The more you read, the better you'll write.

As my top writing coach Zinsser says, "Writing is learned by imitation. If anyone asked me how I learned to write, I'd say I learned by reading the men and women who were doing the kind of writing I wanted to do and trying to figure out how they did it."

Make sure to mix in books on writing, including the great ones such as Zinsser's *On Writing Well* and Roy Peter Clark's *Writing Tools: 55 Essentials for Every Writer*. There is much to be learned in less popular titles, too. Yes, even the ones you find on the discount rack at your local Barnes & Noble.

You may only find one snippet of helpful information in some of the lesser-known books on writing, but that snippet may add another writing hack into your life. You may gain something more valuable than you'd expect..

If it's super dry, apply your 80/20 rule and browse through the chapters for the valuable information.

Try a Standing Desk

Ernest Hemingway wrote standing up, as did Charles Dickens and Winston Churchill. And they did this long before companies began generating revenue on stand-up desks.

I first experimented with one in early 2016, when my wife bought me a simple device that transitioned my standard desk into a stand-up desk. It was a game-changer, not only for my writing but my posture (something I've always bitched at myself for standing poorly, shoulders slumped constantly like most writers at their desks).

Within weeks of that early experience, I purchased a true stand-up desk.

Standing keeps more energy flowing throughout your body over the course of the day and now, I typically spend 95% of my working day on my feet.

Visit my office; there are zero office chairs.

The best writers understand how to hyperactivate their creative zones and remain within peak CUs throughout the day.

And it's all because of the habits they create along the way—habits that keep energy high and the mind and body sharp. You can then spend the time you're saving free of the stress of completing a lingering project.

Next, I'll take you on a journey of a typical, productive writing day with a focus on creative writing and editing.

CHAPTER 10

A DAY IN THE LIFE OF A WRITER

Yep, I totally stole that title from the Beatles. And for this chapter, I also stole an article from myself.

This was originally published on *Search Engine Journal* and entitled "A Day in the Life of a Creative Writer Mad at Google."[9] The idea surfaced when a few readers of my work on various platforms asked me to provide an example of my most productive writing days.

It's a look into the creative side of my writing life, with a focus on optimizing time and productivity over a full day (whether while doing the work or getting away from it to recharge).

The target intended audience was the many blog writers who tap into *Search Engine Journal* daily for inspiration and advice. I love this publication for its wide topic coverage and broad appeal; it isn't a snooty SEO publication, nor does it cater only to digital marketers.

9 https://www.searchenginejournal.com/day-in-life-creative-writer-mad-at-google/312861/

Under editor Danny Goodwin, SEJ began to offer valuable information for a wider audience besides SEOs. The content began speaking to everyone from start-up entrepreneurs to writers to those struggling with everyday business issues.

I began contributing in 2017 and have learned a great deal not only from the editors, but from the audience, as well. I garnered a strong audience of followers who email me questions about writing and productivity.

The piece I offer here didn't win crazy amounts of numbers as far as views or shares are concerned, but the response I received from the readers was intense. Most were writers fed up with SEO and "Google is God" talk.

The following is an excerpt of that article, with tweaks for the everyday writer versus the intended SEO-focused writing crowd that I had originally intended to reach.

Sometimes we just have to walk away from it all. For a man obsessed with productivity and time management, this sentiment is true for making sure we frequently engage in mental relaxation, which helps us think clearer while we're truly at it.

This is true for anybody, especially creatives who spend time creating marketing strategies for writers.

But this time I'm not talking about downtime practices to sustain mental clearness. Rather, I'm talking about walking away from SEO and Google.

I spent over two decades writing for non-digital mediums, and over a decade writing creatively while feeding the Google machine. You have to create content with SEO in mind - especially when businesses rely on me and my team for creating content that will actually rank well in Google.

Besides managing the daily flow of my SEO-driven content marketing agency and one of the leading motorcycle websites, I'm also writing other books, including the one I mentioned early *365 to Vision: Time Management Inverted*, a text on optimizing time management and productivity.

The book's end goal is simple - guide people to finish more quality work in less time, giving people back more of their time to do things they love.

This book writing has freed me from Google. I can't lie; it takes some time to get into a search engine vacation. But once the mind is flowing, it feels heavenly.

I haven't written freely like this for over a decade. I do create many first drafts without an immediate SEO strategy, but writing with SEO in mind is truly ingrained in me, as it is for many content writers that understand the power of SEO.

From keywords to headline tags to worry about crafting the perfect meta description, tactics of writing for a search engine are always there in the back of the mind, just festering like some sickness.

Just as it's good to get away from work to be more productive, I've decided to walk away from thinking about search engines for other forms of writing, which has allowed me to revisit and refresh my creative process.

Following is a typical schedule for creative days - I'll use Tuesdays and Thursdays because they are my typical days for these practices.

The goal is a mind - and schedule - free of distractions and primed to produce the most creative writing possible.

The kind of process that makes your work stand out among a crowd that doesn't like to disrupt the status quo because it's simply comfortable to remain stagnant (*boring*!).

The Evening Before: Set Intentions Before Bed

I typically use Tuesdays and Thursdays for highly creative work. The motivation begins the nights before those days, though, by setting intentions before I go to sleep.

I mean downright imagining them - seeing, hearing, and feeling them. Many self-development gurus discuss this, including Tony Robbins, but the person that explained it simplest for me was Hal Elrod in *The Miracle Morning: The Not-So-Obvious Secret Guaranteed to Transform Your Life Before 8AM* (SEO was definitely not part of that title creation).

Elrod says "The first key to waking up is to remember this: Your first thought in the morning is usually the last thought you had before you went to bed."

The whole point is to awaken and be motivated to write - because if you go to sleep miserable or worry about the writing process itself, your day will start off on a negative note.

This will certainly affect your entire day - especially if you're like many people who have their most creative periods in the early a.m. when the mind is fresh and nothing has robbed any creative bandwidth.

Before going to bed, I meditate and visualize standing at my desk, the windows open, the trees moving, and the words moving across my Mac as I type.

I hear my fingers smashing the keyboard (I'm stupidly loud because of calluses due to wrenching on motorcycles and loving to create a certain cadence), and whatever music I plan for the day. Like most, music selection is important.

I need metal for certain subjects, classical for others, and everything in between, from goth to blues to jazz.

I also imagine what the keyboard feels like, along with the positive emotions I get when I finish something that will add value to another person's life.

This process helps tremendously. Just don't party too much the night before a creative period is scheduled; your evening thoughts may be drastically different from reality, and your day can quickly crumble.

The Morning Of

Now you've awoken with the final thoughts you had before you went to bed, and, though most say it's crazy, your subconscious has already prepped your creativity.

These are the days you wake up to an alarm, preferably from your phone or whatever that's well across your room. The act of getting up and immediately moving helps awaken you quicker, getting the mind energized to produce.

Stretches, meditations, workouts - do whatever you like best to get the energy flowing both physically and creatively.

But the most important thing to do is not check email, text messages, or social media before beginning and ending your first block of time for creative hours.

This is a total life changer, and your mind will be super fresh and sharp and able to deeply focus on your current writing task.

I gave up on office hours years ago and bargained with those I worked with in the past to have at least two at-home days to get my most creative work completed.

But if you have to travel to an office, try to even lose the podcasts or music altogether. Begin the creative process right there in your car - and always keep your phone handy for recording yourself or dictating an email to yourself.

Resist the temptation to check your emails or anything else on your smartphone.

Again, most people have their most creative moments in the morning, but others don't. If this is the case, try to remain unplugged for at least two to three hours before your creative writing period.

And if you have a demanding job where you must check email, resist the temptation of opening anything else but the emails needed for work.

This is why it's vital for companies to be specific with subject lines - sometimes the titles seem urgent, but it's about planning a birthday party or something similar. All will take a bit of your "creative spend," something I previously wrote about in the previous chapter.

Blocks of Distraction-Free Creative Time

Now's the time to get to work within a window of total distraction-free blocked time. Everyone has their personal limits for creativity - some become burnt after 30 minutes, others after five hours.

I've grown mine to about three hours before the mind starts wandering and I lose focus and can't keep my attention creatively directed on my project. Although with practice, as mentioned earlier, I can write five hours straight (sometimes nootropics help!).

A decade ago it was less than an hour, so I made progress but found nothing after say four hours and I am simply writing words, not engaging thoughts.

During this time you must create an environment of zero distractions. This is easy for remote workers, but in-office situations are loaded with distractions that prevent sometimes even two solid hours of creative work from being completed during a normal 40-hour workweek.

For office situations, let coworkers know your creative time periods. And unless someone is dying or the CEO was arrested for fraud, allow no distractions whatsoever.

Keep your cell phone out of sight, and all email/social media/chat notifications off. If you have an office put a sign on the door.

If you're in one of those annoying spaces with an open floor plan where deep thinking is impossible, use headphones and try to super focus as strongly as possible.

When I was working in a noisy marketing department of a pet supplies company year's back, I'd even wear sunglasses to let people know I was not to be bothered.

Do what it takes, but kill the distraction and keep the focus on you creating your best work. Practice zoning out all the noise.

Forget About it, Part 1

Now that you got your most creative period over, it's time to forget about everything you just did and recharge the mind for the next round of blocked time. Check email, social media, text messages, Slack - whatever is needed.

Go bother a coworker, or go for a walk. Read a book. Do whatever is needed to totally clear your mind from your most creative project.

My personal way is by getting on a sportbike and going for a spirited ride - the rides where a single mistake or lack of focus can kill you.

That's the beauty about riding motorcycles at pace - you are forced to not let the mind wander, and must fully focus on the task at hand - riding. If not you can get hurt - and quickly. I have many scars that tell the story, but learned from them and capitalized on them.

And just as creative periods of time are different for everyone, so is the downtime needed to refresh. I may go for a two-hour ride one day, or a 15-minute ride the next. It all depends on the situation.

Just don't get lazy here - it's easy to forget about returning to creative time and just say screw it all for the day.

Sometimes it will happen, and maybe that's your mind telling you it can't take anymore. If so don't brood over it, but discipline yourself to not allow this to happen in the future.

Just before returning to your creative time revisit the meditation practice you did the night before. Prime your mind for another round, and get excited about making a difference through your work.

Remember, the most successful ones are those who don't try to align themselves with the status quo - create something that adds super value, and stand out. High creativity fuels this.

Blocks Distraction-Free Creative Time, Part 2

Once you've recharged, it's time to get back to it. Your mind is fresh now, and depending on how disciplined you are, the workflow will either be as great as the morning session, or much less.

If it's much less, just stick with this and your creative capacity will surely increase. This creativity capacity can be strengthened just like a muscle can - the more discipline you have, the more valuable results you'll have.

Continue what you did in the first part of blocking distraction-free creative time, and go until the limit you're used to.

I also discovered that if I do something ridiculously active during my "Forgot About It" portion above, my afternoon creative blocks are much stronger, and I get more done in less time - my largest goal in life.

Forget About it, Part 2

Once the day's second creative period is over, it's time to once again forget about it. This will refresh your mind for the next day's work, whether that's another creative day or a normal workday with meetings or whatever.

Again, it's completely counterintuitive but the more you get away from it all and just forget about work, the stronger your work becomes.

Your family and friends will also benefit from this downtime because you'll be more focused on the moment, and not discussing work plans every couple of minutes.

Also, before bedtime, don't check emails - my stress levels greatly subsided once I quit checking work emails in the evening.

I was always waiting for that certain reply from a prospective client, or if I got some work in from writers or SEOs.

But the anticipation created more stress than needed - now I don't check email anytime after typically 6 p.m. - unless I'm waiting on something important that needs to be fulfilled for a client or partner.

One of life's biggest secrets to success resides in having patience and discipline. This holds extreme merit for productivity and managing time - especially for those more creative days when the real writing gets done - the writing that moves the proverbial needle.

The steps above have taken me a few years to create, but the patience and discipline to design and implement them for my creative days have truly produced endless ROI.

We only have 1,440 minutes in a day, and we can never get one back - so it pays to truly focus on getting the most out of our creative moments.

Now it's time to spend some of those 1,440 minutes daily on some writing hacks - those hacks that help sustain productivity 365 days a year.

CHAPTER 11

FAVORITE WRITER HACKS

When I tell people I'm a biohacker, some appear stunned while others question what it all means. It's not yet a term that everyone recognizes.

Biohacking as it pertains to my life includes altering my environment to hack my biological makeup, making me think clearly and live stronger and longer.

I discovered the term through Dave Asprey's bulletproof coffee, which uses the C8 strain of MCT coconut oil with grass-fed, unsalted butter to provide all kinds of health benefits and mental clarity. I was skeptical, but tried it back around 2015 and have been on it since. It has helped me run three businesses with complete focus.

I'm not a nutritionist, so I won't get into fats versus carbs versus everything else. What I know is my own experience, and that is that drinking bulletproof coffee worked.

What's more, it inspired me to learn more about my health and how my habits and diet may be affecting my productivity.

It led me to the study and practice of biohacking.

Nowadays, I sleep on a grounding sheets after lying on a acupressure mat for at least 20 minutes; work standing up all day (yes, like Papa) on a grounding mat at a stand-up desk (I don't own an office chair); consume 42 supplements throughout the day; take ice-cold showers; sip lime water constantly; drink celery juice at least six times a week; and take White Mane Mushroom extract that helps increase dreams during REM sleep, to name a few.

Sleeping well is as vital as your awakened lifestyle. Active REM helps us connect the myriad thoughts we have to the work we create which, for you and I, is writing.

When my wife first saw me putting butter in my coffee, filling the bathtub with ice, and walking naked in the backyard as the sun rose to truly soak in the D3, she thought it was different. But then again, she knew she married someone different; someone who, as I've explained, uses writing to get me through life and to help me discover the things I need to explore.

Doctor's reports show I have perfect cholesterol and blood pressure with butter coffee, though I know there's some debate on what's "perfect."

Hacks are a way of life for me and I'll write more about other parts of my regimen soon. I plan to hack my way towards the most quality work in the least amount of time so I can do the best work possible and reclaim more of my time for my family and personal life.

Helping you achieve the same is why I decided to include some of my favorite writing hacks.

Surround Yourself with Those Who Don't Judge

The bulk of the artists I've met over the last 20 years who write, act, paint, or play music are truly unique thinkers.

Especially writers.

If you're true to the craft of writing, you must surround yourself with those who respond well to your mission of discovery through words.

The best writers are on a constant mission to discover knowledge through writing. From poets to playwrights to bloggers, the most successful write to personally discover the meaning of this life, and then revise those words to communicate that meaning and add value to the reader.

Be honest with yourself. Don't put up with the drama of partners and others who don't understand.

It's now 11:38 p.m. on a Wednesday during the peak of COVID-19, and I'm writing.

Down the hall, a few rooms from my office, lies the woman I met shortly after that breakdown at 28. The first thing I did when we got serious was asked her to read the first unpublished novel I had ever written, End Journey (no italics needed because it's mine and only mine...until I'm at least

50 or so!). She read three different drafts of that novel, the first 120,000 words, and the final about 90,000 words.

The characters are absurd. It was written post-9/11 during a time I was working at UPS, doing many drugs, playing music, and simply having a great time with my friends.

The main character, Sam Ralins, still haunts me. That character surfaced over 15 years ago, but still haunts me.

I wanted my girl to understand I was a writer. She read it. And she stayed. Now she's my wife, mother to my son, and business partner.

I don't know if I can stress enough how important it is to surround yourself with people who are positive about your writing. You don't need yes-people to tell you it's perfect, but you absolutely need people in your circle to understand and appreciate your writing process. It'll change your life, and your words will flow smoothly and positively.

What's your favorite music?

Music influenced me to write. A study of Hendrix playing led to reading his lyrical poetry, which led to Bob Dylan, then Jack Kerouac and on from there.

I could easily dedicate an entire novel to the "this artist > this artist > this artist > until I found > this artist."

But Tom Wolfe is the only writer that's allowed to flower his language with symbols. Or wear a white suit. But that's for another study.

Music simply works.

Different forms of music bring drastically different emotions out on the page. And in writing, the more emotion you can bring to the page, the better.

While writing this, I went from Coltrane to Infected Mushroom to 311 to Hendrix to Stevie Ray Vaughan to Phish to G n'R to Breaking Benjamin to Chopin.

For many, music helps words flow. Some, like me, use drastically different music during the various stages of writing.

In each of my three phases of writing—prewriting, writing, and revision—I listen to different tunes. It could be death metal during a pre-writing stage, then swapping to Wes Montgomery for writing, with Lycia for revisions. It could be totally reversed.

During revisions, I may even prefer silence so I can say exactly what I'm reading page-for-page, sentence-for-sentence, work-for-word.

As with so many elements of writing, you need to find what works for you. Just be aware of the impact that music can have on your creativity and make the most of it.

Write About What Makes You Happy

To truly master the craft of the written word, embrace writing that makes you happy—regardless of whether it'll make you money.

Remember, the more you write, the better you'll become.

Write about what you love. For example, my work within the motorcycle industry has never, ever felt like work. I'm obsessed with motorcycles and writing. Pairing the two together has not only delivered endless happiness, but money, also.

But I also like writing poems from the mental notes I take daily of things that are just weird, such as a "For Sale" sign that was notated "Backdoor Living," or a "Closed" sign that says, "No Poopers."

Unlike my motorcycle writings, poetry brings me zero income. But it sure makes me happy, and this happiness refreshes me for the writing that pays the bills.

Commit to Phases of Writing When Fresh

This may change based on who you truly are, and what phase of writing you're committing to at any given moment. Commitment changes whether you're in the drafting stages or the revision stages.

In my 20s, my periods of drafting stages were absurd. Back then, it all happened between midnight and 5 a.m. And so did the editing.

Nowadays, I commit to first drafts while locked away in my office. Some evenings (typically

Wednesdays and Saturdays) I write well into the morning.

With that said, the most serious writing in revisions occurs in the early morning when my brain is freshest.

Find your pockets of optimal writing time, and capitalize on the energy of when your words flow best. Try writing at the same time every day, whether that is before the sun rises, after lunch, or after midnight.

If you train yourself to be ready at the same time every day and that energy arrives, you'll be ready to deliver.

Find what works.

Never get mad at yourself if you end up creating gibberish or just daydreaming. It's all part of the writing process.

Never Wait for Inspiration

Waiting for inspiration is just another form of procrastination. Get writing on a schedule during your most creative moments, when your creative units are at their peak.

Yes, the work is hard. But the tougher the work, the better the final product.

Write Daily and Consistently

In *Outliers*, Malcolm Gladwell argues that becoming truly proficient in anything takes 10,000 hours.

This equates to about 20 hours a week for 10 years.

Writing every day for a consistent amount of time naturally supports that journey to becoming a more proficient writer.

Enforce Downtime

As I said earlier, part of my productivity training demands a strict regime of mandatory downtime. This means truly getting away from anything work-related, from daily periods to a weekly night period to a full day.

Keep your mind fresh for writing. Find your threshold of creativity and get away from it all when words become hard to write or sloppy.

I typically hike, ride a motorcycle, or read a fiction book. These all work for me because it keeps me off the screen. Sometimes these breaks are 15 minutes, but they could be two hours or more depending on what I'm writing.

I've found that it also helps to get away from it all every Wednesday evening, typically from 5 p.m. until I complete my "Miracle Morning" (thanks Hal Elrod!) in the a.m. I don't open emails or think about writing. And one day on the weekend, for an entire day, I do the same.

Longhand Writing

I've mentioned my scribble tablets for long-hand writing before. They are always with me, ready for notes whenever I feel the need.

I love to write in the margins of other books, too. Sometimes I include notes for my son Enzo, so if he decides to study and read like me he'll have a few inspiring notes for himself and future generations.

There's only so much marginal space within a book for jotting down ideas, so my tablet takes care of the rest.

Everything I have ever written since those first poems and lyrics by the railroad tracks as a teenager began in longhand before moving to screen.

Many thoughts nowadays turn into articles for *Forbes*, *Search Engine Journal*, and my business blog. Sometimes it's a three-word sentence that fuels the mind to take off.

There's something unique in beginning all thoughts in longhand. It is intentional and takes time. It's more difficult to completely erase as you go. You think about what you are committing to the page. Give it a try and see how it works for you.

Write Outside of Your Comfort Zone

The more you challenge yourself, the more your brain and writing chops will grow.

I take on unique ghostwriting assignments constantly. I also write blogs for some of my agency's clients a few times per month. Sometimes I know absolutely nothing about the topic and need to do loads of research. Writing outside of my comfort zone forces me to continuously learn, explore, research, and engage.

Just make sure that when you're taking on a new topic, whether on your own or for a client, that you have a great editor with subject matter expertise.

Rewrite Your Favorite Chapters

As I mentioned earlier, Hunter S. Thompson rewrote *The Great Gatsby* and *Farewell to Arms* word-for-word to strengthen his skill.

And it worked; I argue he'd be just as popular as a writer without the Gonzo lifestyle. It was all due to his unmistakable flair and style, which he developed by literally emulating other greats—by typing out their exact words.

Read William Zinsser's *On Writing Well*

Can I mention Zinsser again?

This is one of the most valuable texts on writing. The most important takeaways are the need for constant edits and decluttering your writing from all nonsense and jargon.

In a world where online readers have the smallest attention spans ever, Zinsser's text is needed now more than ever.

For modern freelancers looking to achieve top search engine results, be warned (or smile if you're getting away from it all!) that the word SEO is not mentioned anywhere.

Ask for Criticism

Find someone you trust—a friend, spouse, associate, etc.—and ask them for honest criticism. Be aware; if people are too close they'll outright lie.

You have to assure them that you will take the criticism in the helpful spirit in which it is intended, and actually do that.

Ask them to be honest. Encourage as much trusted criticism as possible. And make sure you learn from it.

Kill the Ego

Keep your ego out of your writing efforts. Writing thick with ego kills the message.

Yes, people do care if you sold the best-selling book on SEO or investing or what have you. But mention it subtly. Create credibility, but don't brag.

Workout

The healthier the body, the healthier the mind, and vice versa.

Get as much exercise as possible. Even walking 1,000 steps a day over 500 can make a drastic difference.

Diet and calmness around booze (coming from a man who LOVES wine) can impact not only your health but your writing in a big way.

Grounding

Shortly after I discovered the standing desk, I discovered grounding.

In the most basic terms, grounding, or earthing, reconnects us with the earth and helps battle inflammation, pain, depression, and fatigue, to name a few.

My first experiment with it was to battle jet lag after landing in Europe to test motorcycles. The first thing I'd do is go to the hotel and walk around barefoot on the grass. I couldn't believe the impact it had on my energy levels, so I tried a grounding mat under my desk, as well. My energy grew, as did my focus.

I have worked barefoot on a grounding mat since. Everyday. All working hours. Now, I have grounding sheets for my bed, too.

The science behind grounding, or earthing, is young, and grows daily. I won't go into crazy amounts of details here. All I know is it assisted me with focus while standing all day and writing. The National Center for Biotechnology Information (NCBI) has some great articles on how grounding improves immunity and inflammation[10], and the U.S. National Library of Medicine (NLM) offers a

---

[10] https://www.ncbi.nlm.nih.gov/pmc/articles/PMC4378297/

great article about how grounding improves mood[11].

One of my clients, Sharon Whiteley, also co-wrote a very informative book on grounding: *Barefoot Wisdom: Better Health Through Grounding*.

Biohacking

Since launching ContentMender, I've obsessed over discovering hacks that can improve my energy and focus. Biohacking is an essential part of my life, and part of my ongoing studies.

The grounding mat and standing desk are just a few elements of my biohacking, along with supplements, ice-cold showers, infrared saunas, Circadian Optics lighting, and more.

Biohacking has helped me produce a consistent flow of content across various industries, some days working for 10-12 hours. I don't get the headaches or mood swings I once did, as my mind remains completely focused.

Above All, Sharpen that Saw Daily

Constantly educating yourself is just as important as a healthy lifestyle.

Make it a habit to do this daily, whether that means listening to an audiobook on the way home from the office, reading for an hour every night, or taking classes.

---

[11] https://pubmed.ncbi.nlm.nih.gov/25748085/

Learning vastly improves your productivity and the more you know, the better suited you are to make decisions.

Reading not only educates you on subject matter, but also for future writing. When you read, you take a bit of that knowledge and style with you. You are what you read, so choose your books wisely.

Read books on writing. Take seminars. Take online SEO classes. Do whatever it takes and *never* stop learning. As I've said before, complacency is the ultimate killer of creativity.

On the topic of learning, I'll end this book with some of the most important books to have in your library. These are my favorites on writing and developing a writer's lifestyle.

CHAPTER 12

MUST-READ BOOKS FOR EVERY WRITER

Everyone is influenced by someone.

For writers, our potential influences are endless. I could list hundreds across all genres, from Hemingway to Don Delillo to Michael Gerber to Richard Koch to Gabriel García Márquez to Adam Grant to Toni Morrison to Chris Bailey to Cal Newport.

I used to gloat about reading five books a month, the selections mixed between classical and postmodern fiction to poetry to business to entrepreneurship to content marketing. Now I read much more, and there's no reason to gloat. I want to learn everything I can about how others write.

Some books offer great lessons through the experiences of others (e.g.: for leadership skills, read Jocko Willink's *Extreme Ownership*!). Others are simply a chance to relax and get away through some journey that the writer discovered and was kind enough to share.

I always add one book a month about the art and discipline of writing into my mix . Some are soon forgotten, but many are revisited over and over again. Here are a few for your own reading list, in no particular order. Some are about writing itself, while others simply offer value for the writer's life in general.

On Writing Well by William S. Zinsser

College wasn't typical for me. And I thank my words for that every day.

While driving the Big Bad Brown truck, I took classes in journalism at a local community college. One teacher, Ed Ackerman, was a columnist for a local paper and delivered a vibe like no other.

He's the one I mentioned who truly belonged in Ivy League schools due to his teaching style. He allowed us students to discover the meaning of our words by writing, rather than trying to force us to understand another's style and simply replicate it.

Ackerman's teaching brought some freedom to the written word that stuck with me throughout my future years in a private school while studying literature. And the bible of Akerman's writing studies was *On Writing Well,* by William Zinsser (I said I'd mention this author again).

Ackerman was the one who told me if there's one book to keep in your bathroom for life, it's *On Writing Well*. Over 20 years later, a copy still resides in my bathroom.

Even after re-reading it numerous times, the lessons of clutter-free writing and simple language and "get people talking" reverberate every time I type.

Read *On Writing Well*. Embrace *On Writing Well*. Re-read *On Writing Well* every year, or the parts you highlight.

Then read Zinsser's next best book, *Writing to Learn*.

Not only will your writing thank you, your readers will, too.

Murder Your Darlings by Roy Peter Clark

Roy Peter Clark solves problems for writers. And if you don't think you actually have writing problems, Clark will help you quickly discover some.

I encountered his work in 2008 after reading *Writing Tools: 50 Essential Strategies for Every Writer*, first published in 2006. The section on "Useful Habits" was beyond useful. I was hooked and couldn't wait for more. I devoured everything he wrote, including his later works *How to Write Short* (2013) and *The Art of X-Ray Reading* (2016). Those two provided lessons for writers, though not as many as *Writing Tools*.

If you're a writer with a full focus on literature, *The Art of X-Ray Reading* will speak more than most books (perhaps not so much to the freelancer looking to make a living with words).

Enter *Murder Your Darlings*, published in January 2020. Clark returns to offering advice for any type of writer, from the journalist to the scholar to the novelist to the blogger.

I read the book in two sittings. The lessons were endless, and as this book is on par with *On Writing Well*, it has been added to my throne collection.

It's that important.

Typical of Clark, he gets deep into not just the mechanics of writing, but the process and philosophical aspects; the latter two by leaning on some of the best literary critics of our time.

He spends an entire chapter discussing Northop Frye's *Fables of Identity: Studies in Poetic Mythology* and the work translates directly to a process that can enhance everyday writing.

One section discusses Frye's thoughts on how we experience music one way, painting another, and literature both ways. Music moves in time, painting moves in space, and literature is presented in both time and space.

When a writer thinks this way, words gratify in more ways than one, helping to develop a new mission to words.

In *Murder Your Darlings*, Clark inspires writers by dissecting 50 great works of writing into simple words that every writer could use. Over and over, he explains the simplicity of the process, and that with hard work we as writers can become better every single day that we dedicate to the not-so-hidden art of writing.

I won't spoil the meaning behind the title "Murder Your Darlings," but it derived from a certain professor thinking much differently about the world in 1914 than we do in 2020 and beyond. Though the principles for writers remain the same.

The book also re-introduced me to the beautiful writing teaching of Don Murray, an author I will speak about in a bit.

The Spooky Art **by Norman Mailer**

Does Norman Mailer need an introduction?

If he does, read *An American Dream*. Then, after you discover the mythical and modern cinema-like scenes, realize it was published in 1965.

His novel-writing career began in 1948 with *The Naked and the Dead*. It ended with *The Castle in the Forest*, published in 2007, the year of his death due to kidney failure at 84-years old.

Mailer's true mastery for writers is his mostly not-discussed and sadly undiscovered for far too long *The Spooky Art: Thoughts on Writing*, published when he was 80-years old in 2003.

By that time, he had written over 30 books and hundreds of articles.

The book is dedicated to J. Michael Lennon, who wrote Mailer's official biography *Norman Mailer: A Double Life* in 2013. Lennon was also Emeritus Professor of English at Wilkes University, the same school where I studied literature during my mid-20s.

Weirdly, I didn't know that fact until I was studying in Wilkes for a year after reading Mailer's book on writing. I met Lennon once but was too embarrassed to talk about literature because I was a bit drunk that morning. Hey, I was 23. I certainly have questions now, and I'll save those for some time in the future.

Back to the book...

My Random House edition runs 308 pages, a typical length for Mailer. And not one word is wasted. Though I hate his thick paragraph style, the content flows.

The three sections that provided the most valuable lessons for me were Craft, Genres and Giants.

The standout in Craft is his perspective on first-person versus third-person, which are "at least as different as major and minor keys in music." He explains that when writing in first person, you "gain immediacy but lose insight." In third person, "you are God" because you can see into everyone's minds.

This is a great lesson for freelancers, whether you write in first person as a ghostwriter for a personality or business, or third for a "know all" perspective.

For many, the second-person voice is more comfortable. And it dilutes the two lessons Mailer teaches from the voice of fiction writing.

The book you're reading now bounces back and forth between first and second person, which is not unusual but worth noting. For most writing that makes money, though, second-person focus with some first-person storytelling works.

Mailer indirectly teaches this.

The chapter Genres explain the relationships we encounter as writers across various disciplines, from journalism to "television" (remember that word!) to film and the "occult," a genius chapter on the "magic" of writing that somehow happens.

Then there is the chapter Giants. One of the most iconic writers of the 20th Century teaches about other icons from his century and the 19th Century, including Hemingway, Twain, D. H. Lawrence, and, of course, Tolstoy.

Even if you never plan to write a word of fiction, read this book. It'll change your perspective on many elements of craft, and more importantly, the art of reading itself.

There's so much to learn through other books! Even if you have never read any of his fiction, stop everything you're doing (including reading this book), and buy *An American Dream*. You'll quickly understand that Mailer was a true master of the written word and has much to teach.

***The Essential Don Murray: Lessons from America's Greatest Teacher*, edited by Thomas Newkirk and Lisa C. Miller**

"The most accurate definition of writing, I believe, is that it is the process of using language to discover meaning in experience and to communicate it."

This is the second time you're reading this quote. I ended my introduction with this quote as well, because it's the ultimate mission of what you and I do as writers. Murray explains this sentiment much better than I ever could. This is exactly why the book of his most cherished writings is a must for writers.

The content focuses on teachers of writing so when reading, have an open mind and think like an educator. This process alone will allow you to explore Murray's multiple lessons on a deeper level. If you're serious about writing, you read everything cover-to-cover. Do this with *The Essential Don Murray*. But first, read Chapter 19, "A Writer's Geography: One Writer at Work."

Murray takes you on a journey of telling a story about writing a story and displays perfectly his thoughts on prewriting, writing, and rewriting, which he coins as "prevision, vision, and revision."

Again, I argue that 80% of writing is experience. This includes scribble tablets and outlines and getting away from it all for fresher creativity. The other 20% is the act of writing itself, which includes first drafts and revisions.

Murray's thoughts on "prevision" correlate, though they are more structured. I learned much from his lessons, including my thoughts on why I failed English in the 11th grade due to "bad writing."

I don't think there was one ounce of discovery throughout writing lessons during most of my high school years, and I'm thankful for that. As I explained earlier, I didn't discover the power of writing until creating words helped me discover what was truly happening in life at 14-years old and on, to today at 40.

Had I read Murray earlier, or been exposed to his teachings, my thoughts would certainly have been different. But then again, I'm glad I discovered his teachings after 20 years of writing and learning by writing. As Mailer points out in the Occult section of *The Spooky Art,* some things happen magically.

It was my time to discover Murray at a certain point in my writing life. Hopefully, your discovery happens much earlier in your writing life. Your readers will thank you.

On Writing: A Memoir of the Craft by Stephen King

I've only made it through three Stephen King novels. I'm not a fan of horror (though I love transgressional fiction), and not a fan of Tolstoy-length novels.

But there's no denying King's status as a prolific writer. As of March 2020, he has penned 57 novels, and all of them have become bestsellers. And I mean best of the bestsellers—he has sold over 350 million books, and is rewarded around $40 million annually for his creations through story-driven writing.

On Writing takes us into the childhood of King and how he became a writer.

Throughout the book, there are invaluable lessons on the craft of writing. King influences you to take a look around in everyday situations to create stories that will keep your readers engaged.

There's much about good-old storytelling and focusing on the audience in this memoir. It can get you eerily inside the head of your readers, something every writer should attempt to achieve. You also learn about the process of prolific writers like King, who demands 2,000 words a day of himself.

He helps to solidify that this thing we do is a process, not something the proverbial muse has to influence. The 365 to Vision concept works more than ever for writers. Be at it every day or go stale.

One of my favorite quotes from King is, "If you want to be a writer, you must do two things above all others: Read a lot and write a lot."

Embrace the writing king's advice and read *On Writing: Memoir of the Craft.*

Other Books That Influence Productivity For the 365 to Vision Writer

These next books have nothing to do with writing pedagogy. They are on everything from entrepreneurship to time management and even include a few fiction books that have influenced me not only to write, but to live.

The 7 Habits of Highly Effective People by Stephen R. Covey

When kids enter high school, their first assignment should focus on reading and writing about Stephen R. Covey's masterpiece: *The 7 Habits of Highly Effective People.*

The lessons can influence highschoolers at a prime age, and act as a prerequisite for any type of college education. When these kids get to college, they should be re-tasked with reading and writing about Covey's book. Yes, it's that important.

Especially for a freelance writer who must create daily habits, 365 days a year, to achieve their ultimate vision of success.

Covey's writing itself is powerful and straightforward (although I wished he used shorter paragraphs). He describes habits as the intersection of:

- Knowledge (what to do and why)
- Skill (how to do it)
- Desire (the want to do, the motivation)

From there, he takes us on a concise ride of the following seven habits in life that take us from being dependent on others to independent to interdependent:

1. Be proactive
2. Begin with the end in mind
3. Put first things first
4. Think win-win
5. Seek first to understand, then to be understood
6. Synergize
7. Sharpen the saw

Putting all these habits into play as a writer will take your level of confidence and skill from zero to full throttle, and quickly.

According to my 2013 edition (original was published in 1989), over 25 million copies were sold. The intro features praise from everyone from Anthony Robbins and Michael Phelps to Tony Hsieh, Steve Young, Steve Forbes, and Seth Godin (the latter one of my all-time favorite writers in the world of marketing—read *Purple Cow* and you'll see why).

Ultimate Sales Machine by Chet Holmes

Back in 2008, I was exposed to blocking time and scheduling days while reading the late Chet Holmes' book, *The Ultimate Sales Machine*. This was by far the most valuable lesson I learned in that book, and it has helped strengthen my focus on time management as a writer.

The book is about winning sales, something I argue every writer can benefit from (especially when first pitching ideas or proposals to editors and book publishers). In fact, Holmes teaches skills worthy of three MBAs.

He begins the book with a chapter on the "Time Management Secrets of Billionaires." It's short, and for me and most writers the most valuable portion of the book. Even if you download or buy the book and read just that chapter, your life will change as a writer. Holmes shows how to implement practices 365 days a year, focusing on elements like making lists, planning the day, and prioritizing tasks.

For writers, the snippets of time management info in chapter one are as vital as learning to cut the clutter. Embrace *The Ultimate Sales Machine*, even if you hate sales.

Hyperfocus by Chris Bailey

No modern thoughts on optimizing productivity and time management 365 days a year are complete without a mention of Chris Bailey and his book *Hyperfocus*.

Bailey sums up the concept of achieving hyperfocus in a single sentence: "Keep one important, complex object of attention in your awareness as you work."

The modern writer must implement this concept daily to achieve daily productivity.

Each lesson Bailey teaches, from disconnecting from electronics entirely to mastering email and meetings to meditation, can help a writer truly discover the meaning of their words and communicate them to their readers in the most valuable way. These lessons help writers complete these tasks daily in the least amount of time, and with the least amount of stress.

Bailey, a Canadian who denied serious job opportunities to experiment with productivity habits such as dicing his smartphone use to an hour a day for three months (all laid out in his debut 2016 book and must-read *The Productivity Project*), also takes his readers in *Hyperfocus* on another journey of "scatterfocus." He dedicates the entire second portion of the book to this concept, which allows the mind to roam intentionally to tap into your creativity.

I've always been a proponent of enforced downtime, which I discussed numerous times throughout this book. And after reading Bailey's thoughts on scatterfocus, his concept helped me focus on this use of letting the mind wander for true creativity more and more.

I'm a huge fan of daydreaming, and taking those breaks daily from "hyperfocus" to "scatterfocus" to help my internal mind clock reset. Bailey's *Hyperfocus* shows you how to do this intelligently. These lessons are timeless for any type of writer who wants to produce daily with full creativity.

Digital Minimalism: Choosing a Focused Life in a Noisy World **by Cal Newport**

If you read Bailey's works, you must follow up with some Cal Newport—especially his *Digital Minimalism: Choosing a Focused Life in a Noisy World.*

Newport is my idea of a productivity philosopher in a world void of distraction. He gets super granular in his book about truly getting away from it all, from smartphones to social media. He becomes a true Jedi of digital minimalism.

The Georgetown University professor, who also wrote another favorite of mine, *Deep Work,* takes readers on a journey of simplicity.

It's a journey that explains why many people don't need to worry about "missing out" on social media, because they are already focused on something that provides more value in their lives.

Though Newport doesn't discuss the writer's life, he speaks directly to the writer. He provides a philosophical approach with real-world lessons of truly detaching from everything digital to create value for not only a writer, but the reader.

As writers, there's ample opportunity to detach from digital and focus on the thoughts with full intention. Newport's *Digital Minimalism* doesn't directly say this, but the work definitely implies it.

On the Road by Jack Kerouac

I didn't read an entire novel until I was 17.

The first was *The Hobbit*. The second, *On the Road*. I went from never reading anything except inserts in tapes and CDs (remember those) to reading Tolkien and then Kerouac.

And when I fell for Kerouac, his lifestyle guided me to make some amazing and not-so-amazing decisions.

The one amazing lesson I took from Kerouac was two-fold: enjoy and experience everything possible, and write about it all.

He schooled me, like Murray taught me decades later, to live life to the fullest and learn from every word.

I can directly correlate all the fiction I wrote in my 20s to Kerouac; close to a million words that began with living life freely and finished with a study in postmodern fiction.

Now, I live and breathe writing or creative writing strategies for companies, from enterprise companies with $20-million market caps to local pest control businesses.

If it wasn't for Dean Moriarity or Sal Paradise, the two main heroes in Kerouac's masterpiece, I would likely still be driving that Big Brown Machine at UPS.

Kerouac teaches flow of words—spontaneous prose as he called it. I trust his spontaneous prose for my spew and outline drafts, to truly pump out words I may or may not understand later.

On the Road helped me understand rambling. And somehow, magically, as Mailer would argue, Kerouac helped me understand the structure of true lifestyle processes.

This structure inadvertently helped me develop time management and productivity studies that lead to a very energetic motorcycle journalist, ghostwriter, entrepreneur, and writer of words about writing itself.

Influence counts. Thank you, Kerouac. I always wanted to say that, from my first trip cross-country as a madman in a Saturn that had a key stuck in the ignition that took me from Pennsylvania to California not once, but twice. And all the stories in between, including the one that made me a writer today.

Kerouac's words changed who I am today. His presence lingers even now. He also helped develop most if not all the writers I discussed in the book, including the man I discuss next, Hunter S. Thompson.

Hell's Angels by Hunter S. Thompson

I'll never forget the first time I read this book.

I was in the Poconos at a high school girlfriend's house. She had finished with college and was teaching at a local grade school there.

The pond outside her home had this awakening smell of freshness in the fall mornings on the weekends I stayed there. In the bedroom, cracked-painted drywall gave way to windows I kept open, allowing those smells to flow through the bedroom.

Upon waking in the early afternoons (hey, I was young), after the sun had baked the water, the smell intensified. I'd awake on those lazy weekends, write for an hour or two, then fish that pond. By 5 p.m., I was typically drunk and would return to the porch to listen to music and read.

One weekend, I spent a Friday and Saturday reading Hunter's *Hell's Angels*. I remember supper being cooked and finished, and all sorts of booze flowing. She passed out, and I continued to read.

I drank that Saturday until around 1 a.m. and finished the book. When I got to the end, I was so mad at Hunter's character I literally stabbed the book seven times.

The blade—a Gerber I still have today and nicknamed "Bateman" for Bret Easton Ellis's character Patrick Bateman—also went through my then-girlfriend's new couch numerous times.

I tried every which way to flip the cushions and patch the hole, but it was impossible. I also had pulled it towards the door to drown it in that fresh-smelling pond, but was too weak (or drunk and stupid) to make it happen.

Regardless, that stabbing of the cushion was symbolic of what good writing does to a person.

I have since reread the same copy (with the knife mark still there) and understand now that his writing style helped direct me more than the actual content of the writing.

This is something Hunter is very good at doing.

He, like my other young influences Kerouac and Bukowski, tells a story in simple language. Yes, they each have unique stories that speak to those 20's lifestyles, but the reason those stories came across so well is because of the simple writing.

Simple writing is difficult. But it moves the reader. That's the first lesson I learned from Hunter. The content was another matter, though I did earn the nickname "Ronzo" from a friend who has never read or heard of Gonzo journalism. Again, as the late Mailer would say, a testament of the Occult. And now here I sit in my "Reality Room," writing words. Simple words to explain lessons in writing.

No fluff.

No reaction without action.

And *Hell's Angels* influenced all of this somehow.

Lunar Park by Bret Easton Ellis

Transgressive fiction. Postmodernism. Words that focus on the mental state of those narrators who need to graphically explore every topic of conversation that most don't want to discuss.

That's my idea of everything from Ellis, and others such as William S. Burroughs and Don Delillo, to name a few drastically different authors who exploit the same ideals in vastly different ways.

But Ellis always stuck out. From the time I read *Less Than Zero* to *American Psycho*, I understood a bit more about true writing. And the writer's process.

Then I read *Lunar Park*, a book that was published in 2005, in 2010. What I discovered was a fiction writer wrapped up in his own characters that talked about that actual writer reminiscing on his own characters much later in life.

Ellis might not have intentionally said much to a practicing writer, but he discusses the process of outlining in Chapter 19 , simply called "the cat":

I was following an outline. I was calculating the weather. I was predicting events. I wanted answers. I needed clarity. I had to control the world.

The writer yearned for chaos, mystery, death. These were his inspirations. This was the impulse he leaned toward. The writer wanted bombs exploding. The writer wanted the Olympian defeat. The writer craved myth and legend and confidence and flames. The writer wanted Patrick Bateman back in our lives. The writer was hoping the horror of it all would galvanize me.

I was at a point where all of what the writer wanted filled me with simple remorse.

(I innocently believed in metaphor, which at this point the writer actively discouraged.)

There were now two opposing strategies for dealing with the current situation.

But the writer was winning, because as I ducked back into the Porsche I could smell a sea wind drifting toward me.

The writer always wins.

For the sake of your own success, I want you to seriously consider writing 365 days a year. Focus on your process, creativity and productivity. My hope in writing this book is that you can take from it the tools, tips, and inspiration you need to move your own writing forward.

The real beauty of writing is in discovery. And I have discovered much while spewing, revising, and editing these words.

I hope you have, too.

Until we meet again...

ABOUT THE AUTHOR

Ron Lieback is the founder and CEO of Content-Mender[12], an SEO-driven content marketing agency based in Northeast Pennsylvania, and online editor at *Ultimate Motorcycling*.[13]. Since the turn of the century, he has written over 15,000 articles across various publications, from *Forbes* to *Search Engine Journal* to *Ultimate Motorcycling*, and has ghostwritten more than 500 articles for CEOs of multi-million-dollar companies.

Lieback resides in Mountain Top, Pa., with his wife Pam and son Enzo. When not writing, he's either riding or wrenching on his collection of motorcy-

---

12 https://contentmender.com/
13 https://ultimatemotorcycling.com/

cles, playing guitar, bumming with the family, or wandering alone in the countryside. He created the "365 to Vision" brand for one main purpose - so people can do more quality work in less time, and truly enjoy every second available within this short life. For more, visit 365toVision.com[14].

[14] https://365tovision.com/

Made in the USA
Las Vegas, NV
13 December 2020

13083218R00129